PreSeNTeD TO a COUraGeOUS GIrL

....

FrOM

....

DaTe

....

100 Extraordinary STORIES for COURAGEOUS Girls

100 Extraordinary STORIES for COURAGEOUS Girls

UNFORGETTABLE TALES OF WOMEN OF FAITH

Jean Fischer

SHILOH kidz

An Imprint of Barbour Publishing, Inc.

Cover design by Emma Segal

Interior illustrations by Heather Burns, Sara Foresti, Isabella Grott, Fabio Mancini, Bonnie Pang, Riley Stark, Lisa Manuzak Wiley, and Rea Zhai

Published by Shiloh Kidz, an imprint of Barbour Publishing, Inc., 1810 Barbour Drive, Uhrichsville, Ohio 44683, www.barbourbooks.com

Our mission is to inspire the world with the life-changing message of the Bible.

ecpa Member of the
Evangelical Christian
Publishers Association

Printed in China.
06189 1018 DS

CONTENTS

ABIGAIL
(1 Samuel 25:1–42)

Abigail Saves the Day

If you lived in Bible times and met Abigail, you might describe her as beautiful, smart, and married to a grumpy, mean man. Why would Abigail marry such a person? It was likely an arranged marriage, meaning that Abigail's father chose Nabal as her husband—probably because Nabal owned land and herds of animals. His wealth meant that Abigail would be well cared for.

One day David, Israel's future king, sent his men to ask Nabal for supplies. In the past, David had been kind to Nabal, and David expected kindness in return, but instead Nabal was rude and sent the men away. This made David so angry he came after Nabal with four hundred soldiers!

When Abigail learned of the foolish thing her husband had done, she sent her servants to David with wine, two hundred loaves of bread, five sheep ready to eat, five baskets of dry grain, one hundred vines of dried grapes, and two hundred pressed cakes of raisins and figs. Then Abigail went to David and apologized for her husband. She urged David not to react with violence to get back at him.

"May thanks be given for your wisdom, and thanks be to you," David said. "You have kept me this day from being guilty of blood, and from punishing with my own hand" (1 Samuel 25:33).

Abigail saved the day. But was Nabal grateful? No. When Abigail got home, she found him selfishly enjoying a feast fit for a king.

We learn from Abigail to bravely stand for what we know is right. Abigail solved the problem by putting her wisdom into action. She did it quietly and in a way that avoided conflict.

What became of Abigail? Shortly after the incident with David, Nabal died. When David heard, he sent Abigail a marriage proposal. . .

And she said, "Yes!"

WHEN SOMEONE DOES SOMETHING BAD TO YOU, DO NOT PAY HIM BACK WITH SOMETHING BAD. TRY TO DO WHAT ALL MEN KNOW IS RIGHT AND GOOD.
ROMANS 12:17

Bessie Adams
(1908–86)

"Bessie, Feed My Sheep"

Before Jesus left the earth to return to His Father in heaven, He told His disciple Peter, "Feed my sheep." Jesus said it three times, so it must have been important. But did Jesus really want Peter to feed a herd of animals?

When Jesus said "sheep," He meant people. Jesus wanted Peter to "feed" His people by reminding them that Jesus had come to save them from sin. Jesus wanted Peter and all Christians to tell the world about Him.

In England during World War II, many years after Jesus went back to heaven, Bessie Adams remembered Jesus' words: "Feed my sheep." And that is exactly what she and her husband did. They brought God's Word, the Bible, to the people.

Bessie and Ken Adams recognized that much of what the people read about Jesus and God was untrue. So they rented a small apartment where they sold Bibles and other true Christian literature.

People were so "hungry" for good books about God that Bessie soon needed a bookstore. She and Ken brought God's Word to soldiers, war prisoners, and many others. Before long they started another bookstore. . .and another. . . and another! By the end of the war, they had opened six bookstores in England. But Bessie and Ken didn't stop there. They began a mission called Christian Literature Crusade (CLC) with the idea to feed God's Word to people all around the world.

Today their mission, CLC, serves fifty-eight countries with more than a thousand men and women continuing to bring true Christian literature to Jesus' "sheep."

Bessie Adams had a good idea, and with God's help it grew into something great!

Do you have a good idea? Tell God about it. Maybe He will help your idea to grow.

. . . .

I AM SURE THAT GOD WHO BEGAN THE GOOD WORK IN YOU WILL
KEEP ON WORKING IN YOU UNTIL THE DAY JESUS CHRIST COMES AGAIN.
PHILIPPIANS 1:6

ANNA
(LUKE 2:21–38)

Anna Shares the Good News

Imagine yourself living in Jerusalem in the years before Jesus' birth. Whenever you entered the temple to pray, you would see Anna. The old woman almost never left the temple. She stayed there day and night praying, sometimes going without food so she could pray even better.

Anna spent most of her life learning God's Word and talking with Him in prayer. She had married as a young woman and lived with her husband for only seven years until he died. Anna remained single the rest of her life, and she turned her attention toward God. She believed with her whole heart what the scriptures said about a Messiah coming to save the world from sin. Anna waited for Him to arrive. Year after year she waited patiently, never doubting.

When Anna was very old, a full eighty-four years after her husband died, she arrived one day to pray at the temple. Something special was happening. A young couple stood dedicating their baby boy to God—promising to raise Him according to God's Word. Standing with them and holding the baby was an old man named Simeon.

The Spirit of God had promised Simeon that he would not die until he saw the Messiah with his own eyes. And now Simeon held baby Jesus, the Messiah! Simeon said, "My eyes have seen the One Who will save men from the punishment of their sins" (Luke 2:30).

Anna heard Simeon. Jesus, the Messiah, had come! She praised and gave thanks to God. Then Anna went out and told the people in Jerusalem about Jesus. She became the first woman ever to share the Good News about Jesus' birth.

Be like Anna. Talk with God every day. Then remember to tell others about Jesus.

I DO EVERYTHING TO SPREAD THE GOOD NEWS AND SHARE IN ITS BLESSINGS.
1 CORINTHIANS 9:23 NLT

ANNIE WALKER ARMSTRONG
(1850–1938)

18,000 Letters

How long does it take to text someone? Not very long, right? Texting is a quick, easy way to communicate a message. But texting did not exist in Annie Walker Armstrong's time. Neither did email. Annie wrote letters—by hand. Long letters. She wrote more than 18,000 letters in one year!

As a young woman living in Baltimore, Annie helped people in need. She shared the Good News that Jesus came to save people from sin so they could live with Him in heaven someday. Annie also prayed for the world's missionaries. But for Annie this wasn't enough. She wanted to do more.

Annie wrote, "If I get hold of an idea which seems to me to be a good one, I somehow do not feel comfortable until I see it carried out." Her good idea was to get women to do more to teach the world about Jesus. To grow her idea, Annie wrote letters that encouraged others to become missionaries and start new churches. In 1888 she organized the Women's Missionary Union (WMU) to help lead and train women in mission work.

If you had to describe Annie with one word, it would be *persistence*. She worked hard and never gave up. Annie died in 1938, but her WMU still exists, encouraging not only women, but men and children too, to tell the world about Jesus. And Annie's name and memory live on through the Annie Armstrong Easter Offering to help support missionaries and their work.

Annie Walker Armstrong reminds us that it takes persistence and hard work to make a good idea grow.

WHATEVER WORK YOU DO, DO IT WITH ALL YOUR HEART. DO IT FOR THE LORD AND NOT FOR MEN.
REMEMBER THAT YOU WILL GET YOUR REWARD FROM THE LORD.
COLOSSIANS 3:23–24

ANNA ASKEW
(1521-46)

✺❧❧❦❦❦❦❦✺

Courageous Anna

Maybe you know someone like Anna Askew. She stood up for her beliefs, and she protected her friends—always!

Born in England during the reign of King Henry VIII, Anna lived in a time of change and trouble. The king arrested people who disobeyed him. He put some to death.

Henry VIII led the Church of England, and he ruled that anyone who did not obey the church's teachings was a traitor—an enemy of his kingdom. Anna did not believe in laws made by the king's church, but only in what the Bible said. She read and memorized the scriptures and taught them to others. When the king ruled that women could not read or teach about the Bible or anything else that disagreed with his religious ideas, Anna disobeyed. She read and talked about the Bible as much as she wanted, and that got her into trouble.

The king's men arrested Anna. They ordered her to take back everything she believed and said about the Bible. But Anna refused. She also would not name her friends who believed as she did that the Bible is the only true Word of God.

For disobeying the king, Anna was tortured and killed—a punishment saved for Henry's worst enemies. Before she died, Anna had one last chance to deny the Bible and her friends. But she would not!

"O Lord," Anna prayed. "I have more enemies now than there be hairs on my head! Yet, Lord. . .I heartily desire. . .that Thou wilt. . .forgive them that violence which they do."

If you had been Anna, would you have given your life to stay true to the Bible and also your friends? Could you forgive your enemies?

• •

STAND FIRM IN THE FAITH. BE COURAGEOUS. BE STRONG.
1 CORINTHIANS 16:13 NLT

Jane Austen
(1775–1817)

Hidden Lessons

When you read a story, do you wonder why the author made the characters do certain things? When you finish a book, do you consider what it taught you? If you dig deep into a story and really think about it, you will find messages that you might have missed. Authors hide lessons in their stories. What happens to characters and how they solve problems can teach you about life.

Jane Austen is one of the most famous eighteenth-century English authors. She was a Christian who hid valuable life lessons in her work. Jane's stories don't usually mention God like the Bible and some other books do; instead, they show how God wants us to live.

If you read Jane's stories, you will discover that her main characters learn good lessons about godly values like honesty, humility—not thinking that you are better than others—and overcoming prejudice. Her characters learn to understand each other better and accept one another just as they are.

Maybe because Jane recognized that God's love is everywhere, she often hid messages about love in her stories.

Growing up the daughter of a minister, Jane knew and loved God. She and her family shared God's love by helping others. While she might not have written boldly about her faith, Jane's faith was strong. When she died, she received the honor of being buried at a famous church (Winchester Cathedral), not because she was an important author, but because she was well known for serving God.

In a prayer, Jane Austen wrote: "[God,] Thou art everywhere present, from Thee no secret can be hid."

Have you discovered life lessons, even lessons about God and love, hidden in the stories you've read?

....

"[GOD] MAKES KNOWN SECRET AND HIDDEN THINGS."
DANIEL 2:22

GLADYS AYLWARD
(1902–70)

Gladys Saves the Children

The time was 1938. The place was China. Gladys Aylward, a missionary from England, was there teaching the Chinese people about Jesus. She had been in the country for eight years, working hard for the Lord, running an inn where drivers of mule teams could rest and enjoy a meal. Gladys shared God's Word with them and anyone else who would listen. She stood up for women's and prisoners' rights, and she took in orphaned children.

Life was good, but China and Japan were now at war, and Gladys had more than a hundred orphans in her care. The Japanese army was coming, planning to take over the place where they lived. They needed to get out! Gladys gathered all the children, and they began walking to a safer place, an orphanage in Sian.

For twelve days they walked, sometimes finding shelter, sometimes hiding on rough mountainsides. Gladys was a tiny woman and worn out from leading the children, but she wouldn't give up, not even when they reached the Yellow River and found no way to cross. All the boats had been hidden to keep the Japanese army from using them.

The children asked, "Why don't we cross?"

"The river is wide and deep. There are no boats," said Gladys.

"Ask God to get us across," the children begged her. "He can do anything!"

So they kneeled and prayed, and soon their prayers were answered! A Chinese officer arrived with boats! Gladys and the children crossed the river. They traveled even farther, and finally, after twenty-eight days, thanks to Gladys and God, they arrived dirty and hungry but safe in Sian.

Gladys's story reminds us that always, and especially when trouble comes, we should put our faith and trust in God. He will provide exactly the kind of help we need.

I WILL LIFT UP MY EYES TO THE MOUNTAINS. WHERE WILL MY HELP COME FROM?
MY HELP COMES FROM THE LORD, WHO MADE HEAVEN AND EARTH.
PSALM 121:1–2

Clara Barton
(1821–1912)

The Shy One

When a disaster happens, you can count on someone coming to help. God is there of course, but He also uses people as helpers. Clara Barton was one of them.

Clara grew up a shy child, but that did not stop her from taking charge when her brother got seriously hurt. "I'll help him get better!" said eleven-year-old Clara. And she did. She stayed home from school for two years caring for David. While she nursed him, Clara discovered she loved helping people.

Her shyness began melting away. When she was just fifteen, Clara became a teacher. She even opened a school. And when the Civil War started, Clara rushed to the combat zone to nurse injured soldiers. Before long people called her the "Angel of the Battlefield." After the war, Clara still helped. She worked to find missing soldiers and reunite them with their families. Clara did not allow shyness to get in her way. She bravely stood up before crowds of people and spoke about helping others.

Clara died more than a hundred years ago, but she continues to help people today. When hurricanes, floods, and other disasters happen, among the first to show up is the American Red Cross. This is because of Clara Barton! She set up the Red Cross in America in 1861 and led it for twenty-three years. Each year in America, the Red Cross responds to many kinds of disasters. They help when just one family needs them or when thousands do.

The shy little girl, Clara Barton, became a woman who learned that helping others was more important than allowing shyness to get in her way.

When you feel a little nervous or shy, ask God to make you His helper. You can count on Him to guide you.

. . . .

FOR GOD DID NOT GIVE US A SPIRIT OF FEAR.
HE GAVE US A SPIRIT OF POWER AND OF LOVE AND OF A GOOD MIND.
2 TIMOTHY 1:7

Margaret Baxter
(1636–81)

A Public-Spirited Woman

Can you name some female leaders? It's common today for women to lead. But that wasn't always true.

When Margaret Baxter lived—in Puritan times—men made the rules. Women were expected to follow them, live quietly, and be happy at home doing household chores. But that wasn't Margaret's style! In her mind, she and her husband were a team, and that caused others to think of her as a "public-spirited woman"—in those days, not a good thing.

Margaret's husband, Henry, was a well-known English preacher and church leader, but he wasn't the quickest at problem solving. He could spend hours thinking about a problem. On the other hand, Margaret could decide right away what was wrong, and she wasn't afraid to tell Henry how to fix it.

It was unusual for a man to take a woman's advice back then, but Henry recognized Margaret's gift for getting to the root of a problem. He said, "Her reasons usually told me that she was in the right." Henry also defended his wife when others accused her of being too busy with church and charities. He reminded them that the apostle Paul had welcomed women to help spread God's Word. Henry called his wife "an artful soul physician." Today we might say she was a wise leader.

You can be a leader too, and nothing can stop you. Look around! Female leaders are everywhere. Think about what you can do at school and wherever you go to set a good example and be a leader among your friends.

LET NO ONE SHOW LITTLE RESPECT FOR YOU BECAUSE YOU ARE YOUNG. SHOW OTHER CHRISTIANS HOW TO LIVE BY YOUR LIFE. THEY SHOULD BE ABLE TO FOLLOW YOU IN THE WAY YOU TALK AND IN WHAT YOU DO.
1 TIMOTHY 4:12

MARY MCLEOD BETHUNE
(1875–1955)

The First Lady of the Struggle

Think about the word *struggle*. If you were wrapped tight like a mummy, would a little wiggle free you? Freeing yourself would take work. And it wouldn't happen right away. To struggle means to fight hard to get free. Struggling takes time, effort, and strength.

Struggle was an everyday word for Mary McLeod Bethune. Born not long after the Civil War, she watched her family and other former slaves struggle to make a life free from slavery. Mary's mom continued to work for her former owner until she earned enough money to buy the land where the family grew cotton. Maybe it was her mother's strong example combined with faith in God that made Mary work extra hard.

African-American children were finally free to attend school. When a missionary opened a school in her area, Mary walked miles to go there and learn. And learn she did! She grew up to graduate from college and become a teacher. But that wasn't enough. She wanted to provide the best education for all African-American children, so she rented a tiny cottage and opened a school. At first she had six students. Then more came. And more. Mary's school grew and grew.

Mary recognized that African-Americans struggled to enjoy the same freedoms white people did. For the rest of her life, she worked to help them gain equality. Her hard work got the attention of many, especially President Franklin D. Roosevelt. He chose her as his adviser to help bring all Americans together as equals, whatever the color of their skin. Soon Mary became known as a great leader, "The First Lady of the Struggle."

What can you learn from Mary's story? When you see people struggling, help them. God wants everyone set free. Ask Him to help you help others.

• •

HONOR AND THANKS BE TO THE LORD, WHO CARRIES OUR HEAVY LOADS DAY BY DAY.
HE IS THE GOD WHO SAVES US. OUR GOD IS A GOD WHO SETS US FREE.
PSALM 68:19–20

SAINT BLANDINA
(162–177)

"I Am a Christian!"

Why was Jesus hated and crucified? Because He said He came from God and that He *was* God, but many didn't believe Him. They killed Jesus because they thought He was fake—that He was disrespecting God and His holy scriptures. We know that's not true. Jesus was, and is, exactly who He said He was: the Son of God, our Savior who came to save us from sin.

Hatred continued as more people came to believe in Jesus. Blandina's story happened long ago in France, at a time when Christians were hated and forced to give up their businesses and houses. Mobs beat them and robbed them. Many were arrested.

Blandina was a slave, only fifteen years old, when she and her master were arrested for being Christians. She and all those arrested with her were given a chance to turn against Jesus, but Blandina refused. The rulers put her in the worst part of their ancient prison, and they tortured her in every way they could think of. What they did to her was awful—and still Blandina said, "I am a Christian!"

A holiday was near, a day to celebrate Rome and its emperor. The citizens planned to gather at the stadium to enjoy some entertainment—professional fighters, boxers, and wrestlers. But it cost money to hire them. So the rulers decided it would be "entertaining" for the citizens to watch Christians being killed by wild animals. When the day of celebration arrived, Blandina was taken into the stadium and killed by a wild bull. But she never lost faith in her Lord. She said again and again, "I am a Christian, and we've done nothing wrong."

The story of Blandina's life is not a happy one, but it's a story of amazing courage and faith.

WHEN I AM AFRAID, I WILL TRUST YOU. I PRAISE GOD FOR HIS WORD.
I TRUST GOD, SO I AM NOT AFRAID. WHAT CAN HUMAN BEINGS DO TO ME?
PSALM 56:3–4 NCV

Catherine Booth
(1829–90)

Catherine, Mother of an Army

Catherine Booth grew up in England in the 1800s, a time before television, computers, video games, phones, and everything else electronic. When she was a teen, a spine injury forced her to stay in bed for months. To keep busy, Catherine read. Most of the books were about God, and as she learned more about Him, Catherine wanted to tell everyone about Jesus. She felt God calling her to preach. But there was a problem.

"A woman's place is in the home." That's what many people believed, and women were not welcome as ministers. Catherine argued that God saw men and women as equals, one not better than the other. She wouldn't give up her calling to share with others that Jesus came to save them from sin.

Catherine fell in love. She married a young preacher, William Booth. "I would not stop a woman preaching," he said. So Catherine preached! She preached in her husband's church and wherever she was welcome. Many accepted Jesus as their Savior because of Catherine's words.

William and Catherine set up tents in London where they preached to all who would listen. Their ministry grew. They taught others to lead people to Jesus, and soon they had more than a thousand volunteers. William called this group of helpers the "Salvation Army." Together he and Catherine were its leaders, and she became known as the "Army Mother."

Today the Salvation Army serves in more than a hundred countries! You see its workers ringing bells near stores at Christmastime, raising money to help people in need. The next time you see them, think of Catherine Booth, and remember that everyone is equal in God's eyes. He calls men, women, boys, and girls to do His work.

THEN PETER SAID, "I CAN SEE, FOR SURE, THAT GOD DOES NOT RESPECT ONE PERSON MORE THAN ANOTHER."
ACTS 10:34

EVELYN "EVIE" BRAND
(1879–1974)

❧~∾∾∾∾∾~❧

"God, Give Me Another Mountain"

Imagine living in London in the early 1900s. You fall madly in love with a handsome young man named Jesse. "Will you marry me?" he asks. Of course you will! He lives in India, and you go to be with him. After the I-dos, you and your husband head home. There are no roads. It's pouring rain. You hike toward the mountains into the hills until you arrive at his house, a tiny three-room shack.

That's how Evie Brand's marriage began. But she didn't mind. Evie and Jesse were missionaries serving poor people in a place called "the mountains of death."

The people there were sick. Malaria—a deadly disease carried by mosquitoes—killed many. For more than twenty-five years, Evie and Jesse did their best to help the mountain people get well. They also shared God's Word with them and started a church. But then something awful happened. Jesse got malaria and died. Evie was heartbroken! The love of her life was gone. Their two children, Connie and Paul, were in school in England. She was alone.

Evie could have given up and returned to London, but she didn't. Instead, she asked God to help her do even more. "God, give me another mountain," she prayed.

For the rest of her life, Evie stayed in India helping the mountain people. Always, she relied on God to keep her mentally and physically strong. She grew old. Still that didn't stop "Granny Brand" from doing God's work. "I am just [an]. . .old. . .weak woman," she said. "God. . .gives me the strength I need each day."

Evie died at age ninety-five, still working for God.

When things get hard, remember Evie. Trust that God will keep you strong every day of your life.

∙∙

I CAN DO ALL THINGS BECAUSE CHRIST GIVES ME THE STRENGTH.
PHILIPPIANS 4:13

ESTHER EDWARDS BURR
(1732–58)

❧❦❧

Best Friends

Do you like to write? Esther Burr did. In a time long before computers made writing easy, Esther journaled and wrote letters. Although she lived almost three hundred years ago, her letters and journals still exist. From reading them, we can learn about true friendship.

Esther's best friend, Sarah, lived too far away to visit in person. There were no cars, planes, or trains then. People relied on horses, and travel took a long time. The two women wrote letters to each other.

Her friendship with Sarah, according to Esther, was a gift from God, one that would last forever. Today we would say the two were BFFs, but in her journal, Esther said it this way: "True friendship is first inkindled by a spark from Heaven, and heaven will never suffer it to go out, but it will burn to all Eternity."

Esther could tell Sarah anything and trust that Sarah wouldn't share it. Esther believed we should be able to trust a friend with a secret. In another journal entry, she wrote: "Whatsoever had been spoken in Confidence whiles there was supposed to be a friendship aught to be kept secret."

Sarah was so trustworthy that she burned any letter from Esther that contained a secret.

When Esther didn't have a friend in her town who would talk with her about Jesus, she knew she could write about Him to Sarah. Both were Christians who loved the Lord, and they openly shared their faith with each other.

The two friends wrote more than a hundred letters before Esther died of a fever, sadly at age twenty-six.

Think about your best friend. Is she or he a true friend? Can you trust that person with anything? Can you talk openly with each other about God?

• •

A FRIEND LOVES YOU ALL THE TIME.
PROVERBS 17:17 NCV

MILDRED CABLE
(1878–1952)

The Trio

Missionaries are modern-day disciples traveling the world. They share the Good News that Jesus came to save us from sin so someday we can live forever in heaven.

While in England at age twenty-two, Mildred Cable felt God leading her to mission work in China. She went and became a teacher at a girls' school. There she met two sisters, Evangeline and Francesca French. The three taught together for twenty-one years, becoming known as "The Trio."

You might think by the time The Trio were in their forties they were settled in their work. Not so! They wanted to do more. People living in remote areas of the Gobi Desert hadn't heard about Jesus, so The Trio decided to tell them.

They were like pioneers with Mildred leading them. Danger lurked every-where! The desert spanned a thousand lonely and mostly treeless miles. Nights, bitter cold. Days, beastly hot. Still, traveling in a rough, wooden cart, the women reached faraway villages to talk about Jesus. They held Sunday school for the children; then the children went home and taught their parents what they learned. Wherever The Trio went, the Good News spread. People came to know Jesus and invite Him into their hearts as Savior.

The Trio made five trips across the desert. When they revisited a village, they saw God at work—people accepting Jesus as Savior and wanting to know more about Him.

Mildred and The Trio's story reminds us that it's not easy being a missionary. She wrote to those considering mission work, "We need scarcely remind you that many incidents which are romantic and faith-inspiring when viewed from a dis-tance are wrought out in circumstances when loyalty is tested to the uttermost."

Isn't it great that God trusts us to do His work even when we face difficult circumstances?

BUT HOW CAN THEY CALL ON HIM IF THEY HAVE NOT PUT THEIR TRUST IN HIM?
AND HOW CAN THEY PUT THEIR TRUST IN HIM IF THEY HAVE NOT HEARD OF HIM?
ROMANS 10:14

AMY Carmichael
(1867–1951)

Amma Amy

Do you know someone your age who reaches out to help others? Maybe you are that kid! You see a classmate or friend in need, and you rush in to help.

Amy Carmichael was like that. As a teenager, she saw girls her age who needed hope. These girls, known as the "shawlies," worked in the flour mills in Belfast, Ireland, where Amy lived. They were poor and hungry, and they needed to know Jesus.

When Amy set up Bible studies at a local church, some of its members were unhappy. They didn't want the shawlies there. But Amy didn't care. She knew God welcomes every child into His house. God blessed Amy's work, and she was able to buy a building to church hundreds of girls who wanted to learn about Jesus.

Amy could have stayed there, ministering to the girls in Ireland, but God wanted her somewhere else—in India!

It was hard. She had to learn a new language and earn the people's trust. Soon, just like in Ireland, girls began showing up to learn about the Lord. More came, kids of all ages, kids without families who needed a home. Before long Amy had more than fifty children to care for. They called her "Amma," which in their language means "mother." Being mother to all those kids was hard work, but God provided everything Amy needed.

For fifty-five years, Amy stayed in India caring for children. She was quiet about her work. She didn't even want a gravestone marking her grave when she died. When she passed away at age eighty-three, the children used a birdbath to mark her grave. On it was carved the word AMMA.

Look around you today for a kid in need. Be like Amy and see what you can do to help.

"I TELL YOU, MY FATHER IN HEAVEN DOES NOT WANT ONE OF THESE LITTLE CHILDREN TO BE LOST."
MATTHEW 18:14

Fanny Crosby
(1820–1915)

Girl with an Attitude

Oh, what a happy soul I am,
Although I cannot see!
I am resolved that in this world
Contented I will be.

How many blessings I enjoy
That other people don't,
To weep and sigh because I'm blind
I cannot, and I won't!

Eight-year-old Fanny Crosby wrote that poem. Yes, she was blind, but she wouldn't allow blindness to make her sad. Instead, she chose to have a positive attitude.

Fanny loved writing poems. She also enjoyed memorizing the Bible—several chapters a week. At age fifteen she left home to attend a school for the blind in New York City.

The New York Institute for the Blind is where Fanny stayed for twenty-three years, not only as a student, but later as a teacher. Everyone around her noticed that Fanny had a talent for writing poetry. Her writing led her to meet famous people, including presidents and governors. She even read one of her poems in the United States Senate chamber in Washington, DC.

Fanny's poems were published in books, but none made her famous. Fame arrived when she began writing lyrics for Sunday school songs and hymns. Soon almost everyone knew her name.

Always she asked God to provide her with ideas for her songs. The ideas came! In her lifetime, Fanny Crosby wrote lyrics for nearly nine thousand songs.

All her life Fanny kept a positive attitude. She even thanked God for her blindness. "If perfect earthly sight were offered me tomorrow, I would not accept it," she said. "I might not have sung hymns to the praise of God if I had been distracted by the beautiful and interesting things about me."

Whenever you feel sorry for yourself, turn it around. Remember Fanny. Put on a positive attitude and sing a song of praise to God.

. . . .

A GLAD HEART IS GOOD MEDICINE, BUT A BROKEN SPIRIT DRIES UP THE BONES.
PROVERBS 17:22

DEBORAH
(JUDGES 4–5)

Deborah, a Mother for Israel

In Bible times, Deborah was Israel's only female judge. She was a fair judge who trusted God. And God trusted Deborah with a dangerous mission: to free the Israelites from the control of Canaan's cruel King Jabin.

The king's gigantic army with its nine hundred chariots terrified the Israelites. So they did nothing but suffer under the king's rule. God didn't want that. He wanted His people freed from the king's evil ways.

God often spoke through Deborah to the people of Israel. One day He gave her a message for a man named Barak: "Call out 10,000 warriors. . . . I will call out Sisera, commander of Jabin's army, along with his chariots and warriors. . . . I will give you victory over him" (Judges 4:6–7 NLT).

But Barak was afraid. "I will go, but only if you go with me," he told Deborah (verse 8 NLT).

"I will go with you," she answered bravely. "But you will not get credit for the victory. The Lord will let a woman defeat Sisera" (verse 9 NCV).

So they went, Deborah, Barak, and the Israelite soldiers. "The Lord has already cleared the way," Deborah told them (verse 14 NCV).

When the battle against Sisera and his soldiers began, God did something great. He made the king's army panic. Barak and his warriors chased the nine hundred chariots until all the king's soldiers died. And what about their leader, Sisera? He ran away and hid in the tent of a woman named Jael. It was Jael who killed him, the last of the king's evil men. Finally, the Israelites became free from Jabin's rule, and peace was with them and their land.

Deborah had been like a mom caring for her kids. She faced danger to keep the Israelites safe from a bad king.

Are you brave like Deborah? Whenever you need courage, ask God. He will help you.

"BE STRONG AND COURAGEOUS, AND DO THE WORK. DON'T BE AFRAID OR DISCOURAGED, FOR THE Lord GOD, MY GOD, IS WITH YOU."
1 Chronicles 28:20 NLT

ELISABETH DIRKS
(DIED 1552)

❧∗❀❀❀∗❀❀❀∗❀∗

She Wouldn't Give Up!

Elisabeth Dirks was a Christian martyr (pronounced *mar-ter*), a person killed for teaching others about Jesus. In the Bible's New Testament, you will find stories of other martyrs. John the Baptist, Stephen, James—these are just a few of Jesus' followers who were killed because of their faith. Elisabeth's story comes later, after the Bible was written. She lived during the 1500s.

Elisabeth's parents sent her to live in a convent school at a time when the Catholic Church was thought to be the only true church. Not everyone felt that way. Some pulled away from the church because they didn't believe everything it taught. After studying the Bible, Elisabeth decided she agreed with those people. She ran away from the convent and joined others who disagreed with the Catholic Church's teachings. Elisabeth became one of the group's first female ministers, and she was never shy about sharing her beliefs.

For Elisabeth, Jesus came first. Nobody was going to stop her from teaching others what she believed about Him, and that got her into trouble. The authorities arrested Elisabeth for what they said were lies about Jesus. They wanted her to name others in her group so they could arrest them too. But Elisabeth wouldn't. Instead, she told them what she believed to be true about Jesus, and that made them angry. They threatened to torture her if she didn't tell. But Elisabeth refused.

Elisabeth suffered terribly. When she would not give up her friends or her beliefs about Jesus, she was killed—drowned—by those who disagreed.

Elisabeth's story isn't a happy one, but it holds two powerful lessons. Be like Elisabeth. Stand up for Jesus, no matter what. And unlike the men who killed her, be respectful toward those who believe differently than you.

JESUS SAID TO HIS FOLLOWERS, "IF ANYONE WANTS TO BE MY FOLLOWER, HE MUST FORGET ABOUT HIMSELF. HE MUST TAKE UP HIS CROSS AND FOLLOW ME."
MATTHEW 16:24

Dorcas
(ACTS 9:36–43)

The Dressmaker

Many came to believe in Jesus because of His disciples. Peter and others traveled to cities and towns spreading the Good News that Jesus had come to save the world from sin. Everywhere men, women, and children prayed and asked Jesus to come into their hearts.

One of those women was Dorcas. The people of Joppa, the seaside city where she lived, called her by another name: Tabitha. They knew her as a Jesus follower. Jesus' love shone through her as she did many good deeds and acts of kindness, mainly for the poor.

Dorcas had a special talent—sewing beautiful clothing. She could have sold her clothing to the rich, but instead she gave it to the poor. Women who had nothing and were alone caring for their families, those whose husbands had died, wore Dorcas's beautiful clothes.

One day Dorcas became sick and died. The women in Joppa cried and mourned, but then they remembered that Jesus' disciple Peter was in a nearby town. They sent for him, and Peter came at once. He went to the room where Dorcas's body lay, and he sent the women away.

Peter got on his knees and prayed for a miracle. "Tabitha, get up!" he said (Acts 9:40). God answered Peter's prayer. Dorcas opened her eyes and sat up. Peter invited the women back into the room, and they could hardly believe their eyes when they saw Dorcas standing and alive! News of this spread through Joppa, and because of it many more people put their trust in Jesus as Savior.

The important lesson in Dorcas's story isn't that she was raised from the dead, but instead that she served God with her many acts of kindness.

Can you use your special talents to help others? How can you be kind today?

. . . .

GOD ALWAYS DOES WHAT IS RIGHT. HE WILL NOT FORGET THE WORK YOU DID TO HELP THE CHRISTIANS AND THE WORK YOU ARE STILL DOING TO HELP THEM. THIS SHOWS YOUR LOVE FOR CHRIST.
HEBREWS 6:10

Emma Dryer
(1835–1925)

She Gave Up All for God

Something awful happened when Emeline Dryer was a little girl: her parents died.

God blessed Emma with an aunt who took her in and raised her. They lived in New York, and the city held great opportunities for Emma. She went to the best schools. From elementary school through college, Emma earned excellent grades. She became a teacher, first at an elementary school, then at a college. Emma was well paid and popular. But then she gave it all up! Why? Because God had another plan for her.

God put the idea in Emma's heart to teach others about Jesus. More than a job and salary that made her comfortable, Emma wanted to obey God. So she left the college and set out to do His work.

Emma moved to Chicago where she met a preacher, D. L. Moody, who spoke to large crowds, teaching them about Jesus. Mr. Moody admired Emma's teaching skills and her strong Christian faith. He encouraged her to start a training school for missionaries. It would be the missionaries' jobs to go to the homes of people who didn't know Jesus and tell about Him.

With Emma in charge, the school grew. Many learned to love Jesus. Then those people taught their children about Jesus and raised them to be Christian men and women.

Emma died at an old age in 1925, still serving God. All these years later, her school, Moody Bible Institute, continues to exist in Chicago, training others to do God's work. Emma gave up everything to help God work His plan. She was left with not a lot of money, but she always had enough to live a good, happy life.

We learn from her story that when we choose to serve God, He gives us exactly what we need.

AND MY GOD WILL GIVE YOU EVERYTHING YOU NEED BECAUSE OF HIS GREAT RICHES IN CHRIST JESUS.
PHILIPPIANS 4:19

ANNE DUTTON
(1692–1765)

The Private Servant

Today women serve God in many ways. Some are missionaries, while others teach classes in churches and Sunday schools. Do you know a female pastor? There are many female pastors today. Women are free to serve God however they choose. But that wasn't always true. When Anne Dutton lived, men held the important roles serving God. Women helped but rarely led.

Anne was a wise woman who loved sharing God with others. If someone needed advice, she often knew what to say. Her talent was writing about God and His greatness. But Anne worried about her writing. She didn't worry that it wasn't good enough. Instead, she was concerned about whether she should be writing at all. Most men, and many women too, felt it was wrong for a woman to be an author—to publish anything that focused attention on herself.

After thinking about it, Anne decided she didn't write about God to focus attention on *her*. She wrote to focus attention on *Him*! So she wrote. Anne wrote booklets, poems, letters, and hymns about God. But she wrote them to be shared privately, not as part of public worship.

She bravely did what she knew was right. Anne used her talent to serve God. She wrote to lead others closer to Him. You probably won't see Anne Dutton's name today among the many famous women who served God. She went about her work quietly. But in a time when women were discouraged from serving God in public, she found a way to serve. Because of her writing, others came to know and love God.

Maybe you don't like being in the spotlight. Maybe serving God publicly isn't your thing. That's okay. Ask God how you can serve Him quietly. He's ready to give you an answer.

"LET YOUR LIGHT SHINE IN FRONT OF MEN. THEN THEY WILL SEE THE GOOD THINGS YOU DO AND WILL HONOR YOUR FATHER WHO IS IN HEAVEN."
MATTHEW 5:15–16

SARAH PIERPOINT EDWARDS
(1710-58)

A Good Wife and Mother

When you read the Bible, you will find many stories about kings. Some were bad kings. Others good. Most are written about in history books. But one king is mentioned in the Bible just once. His name was King Lemuel, and he's found in the book of Proverbs, chapter 31. Nothing is written about him. Instead, we read his mother's advice to him about choosing a wife. Read Proverbs 31:10–31, and you will discover some of the things a good wife and mother does. One is that she works very hard caring for her family.

Sarah Edwards is remembered as an example of a good wife and mother. She lived in the early American colonies where she married a famous minister, Jonathan Edwards. He could be difficult, but Sarah stuck by him and helped him become the best he could be.

The work of raising their eleven children mostly fell on Sarah. Along with managing the house, she also homeschooled her children. She taught them the important subjects, and she made sure they knew God. If she had to punish one of her kids, Sarah did it gently, quietly, and always with love.

Sarah was a good mom who had no idea of the effect her parenting would have on the world. Her children's love for God led them all either to become or marry a minister. Her many great-grandchildren included pastors, teachers, lawyers, doctors, business owners, judges, mayors, senators, and even a United States vice president! In a biography about Sarah, author Elisabeth Dodds wrote, "Has any other mother contributed more. . .to the leadership of a nation?"

Now think about your mom or another woman who helps to raise you. How has she made you a better person? Have you told her what she means to you and thanked her?

. . . .

SHE SPEAKS WISE WORDS AND TEACHES OTHERS TO BE KIND. SHE WATCHES OVER HER FAMILY AND NEVER WASTES HER TIME. HER CHILDREN SPEAK WELL OF HER. HER HUSBAND ALSO PRAISES HER.
PROVERBS 31:26–28 NCV

ELIZABETH
(LUKE 1)

She Trusted God

If you know the story of Jesus' birth, you know that Mary was surprised when an angel told her she would give birth to Jesus, the miracle baby sent from God.

But Jesus wasn't the only miracle baby born around that time. Mary's older cousin, Elizabeth, was going to have a baby too. And *she* was surprised! Elizabeth was an old woman—much too old to have a baby. Still, it was true.

God was putting together a wonderful plan.

An angel had visited Elizabeth's husband, Zechariah. The angel said Elizabeth would have a baby boy whom they should name John. He would be great in the sight of God, he would love God, and he would introduce Jesus to the world. Zechariah didn't believe the angel because women Elizabeth's age just didn't have babies! But Elizabeth believed. Although she didn't know God's plan, she trusted that He had one—a *good* one. She was going to have a baby!

When Mary found out about Elizabeth's baby, she hurried to visit and tell her that they both were going to have sons. What happy news! Elizabeth told Mary, "You are happy because you believed. Everything will happen as the Lord told you it would happen" (Luke 1:45). Elizabeth had faith.

Baby John arrived about six months before Jesus was born. God already had a plan for him. He would grow up to be John the Baptist, the prophet who spoke about God's Son and made people ready to meet Him.

Jesus' and John's mothers both believed what God's angel said. And both miracles happened! They were part of God's plan.

Are you like Elizabeth and Mary? Do you trust God to have a good plan for you even when it's hard to believe?

· ·

"FOR I KNOW THE PLANS I HAVE FOR YOU," SAYS THE LORD, "PLANS FOR
WELL-BEING AND NOT FOR TROUBLE, TO GIVE YOU A FUTURE AND A HOPE."
JEREMIAH 29:11

ELISABETH ELLIOT
(1926–2015)

≈∂∂∂⌐⌐⌐≈

Elisabeth, the Brave One

What does it mean to be brave? Maybe you think bravery is doing something dangerous, like mountain climbing. Some brave people risk their lives to save others. Fighting an illness like cancer is also brave. But have you ever thought that forgiving someone can be brave?

Elisabeth Elliot's story is about a brave kind of forgiveness. It begins in Ecuador in the 1950s when Elisabeth and her husband, Jim, were missionaries there.

Jim's hope was to tell everyone about Jesus, especially a tribe living by themselves deep in the jungle. The Aucas didn't trust anyone who came into their territory. They murdered intruders. But Jim and several other missionaries managed to become their friends—at least, that's what they thought. Suddenly the Aucas turned against the five missionary men and killed them with spears.

You might imagine that after that Elisabeth would want nothing to do with the Aucas. But instead, she stayed in Ecuador and lived with another tribe near them. There she met two Auca women who became her friends. They trusted Elisabeth, and before long she was invited to live with the Aucas, the tribe that had killed her husband. Elisabeth lived with them peacefully and shared with them God's Word, the Bible. Because of her, many came to know Jesus as their Savior.

Elisabeth believed that God had called her to forgive the Aucas and continue to minister to them. God *did* use Elisabeth! Because of her forgiveness, the Aucas learned that Jesus came and died to forgive them—and everyone—of their sins.

Elisabeth and Jim are both examples of what it means to be brave. They risked their lives to save the Aucas from certain death. Because of their bravery and Elisabeth's forgiveness, many of the Aucas will enjoy life in heaven forever.

· ·

"BUT TO YOU WHO ARE WILLING TO LISTEN, I SAY, LOVE YOUR ENEMIES!
DO GOOD TO THOSE WHO HATE YOU."
LUKE 6:27 NLT

ESTHER
(ESTHER 2:1–9:25)

The Queen's Secret

Queen Esther kept a secret from her husband: she was Jewish. The king thought his wife was Persian like the other women in his kingdom. He disliked Jews, and if he had known, he might not have married Esther.

Esther's older cousin, a Jewish man named Mordecai, had raised Esther after her parents died. The only way Mordecai could see Esther and keep her secret was to pretend they weren't related. He often hung around the castle gate to get a glimpse of Esther to be sure she was okay.

One day an evil man named Haman ordered Mordecai to bow to him, but Mordecai refused. He would bow only to God. That made Haman angry. He went to the king. "Jews are terrible people," he said. He convinced the king to order that all the Jews be killed.

Mordecai got a message to Esther. He told her what was going on.

I have to tell my husband that I'm Jewish, Esther thought. *I must convince him not to kill the Jewish people.* She sent Mordecai a message: "Pray for me. I will go in to the king, which is against the law. And if I die, I die."

It was a scary thing, but Esther confessed the truth to the king. She also told him that she and Mordecai were related.

Her husband knew Mordecai! In fact, he owed Mordecai his life because Mordecai had told him when he heard men plotting to kill the king.

The king's attitude about murdering the Jews changed. All their lives were spared, thanks to Esther telling the truth.

Have you ever been afraid to tell the truth? Don't be. It's the right thing to do. When you tell the truth, you can be sure God is on your side.

THE LORD HATES LYING LIPS, BUT THOSE WHO SPEAK THE TRUTH ARE HIS JOY.
PROVERBS 12:22

Eve
(GENESIS 2:4–3:24)

Eve's Big Mistake

We learn important lessons from our own mistakes and also from the mistakes of others. Eve's story is about a mistake that changed the world forever.

When God created the earth, He made everything perfect. He made a perfect man, Adam, to live on earth, and God created a lovely garden called Eden where Adam could live. God put all kinds of beautiful trees with delicious fruit there. At the center of the garden, He set a special tree, the tree of learning about good and evil. God didn't want Adam to know about evil things, so He ordered Adam never to eat fruit from that tree. Next, God created a perfect woman as a helper for Adam. She was Eve.

Eve felt curious about that center tree in the garden. She was even more curious when a sneaky snake told her that eating fruit from the tree would make her like God, knowing both good and evil. The Bible says, "The woman saw that the tree was good for food, and pleasing to the eyes, and could fill the desire of making one wise. So she took of its fruit and ate. She also gave some to her husband, and he ate" (Genesis 3:6).

It was the worst mistake ever! Eating that fruit opened their eyes to everything evil and allowed sin to enter the world. Eve's mistake, disobeying God, changed the world forever. Can you imagine if everyone had stayed perfect and obeyed God? Earth would be heaven!

Eve's mistake reminds us to obey God and do what is right.

Remember, God loves us even though we aren't perfect. He sent Jesus to forgive our sins so that someday we can live with Him in heaven.

Think about it. What have you learned from your mistakes?

"DO NOT LET US BE TEMPTED, BUT KEEP US FROM SIN."
MATTHEW 6:13

ELIZABETH FRY
(1780–1845)

The Prison Angel

As a young girl growing up in England, Elizabeth Fry had no idea what it was like being poor. Her father, a banker, gave his children everything they needed and more.

Elizabeth had a kind heart and concern for the poor. When she was in her teens, Elizabeth compared her life to theirs, and she wondered if God existed. God knew what she was thinking! He put the idea in Elizabeth's heart to do something to help.

She began by making clothes for poor people. Back then children worked hard in factories to earn a little money for their families. Elizabeth started a Sunday school for them and taught them to read.

As an adult, she began visiting the poor in their houses. The conditions were shocking! Elizabeth did what she could to help, but she felt it wasn't enough.

God had a plan for her. He led her to visit a women's prison, and when Elizabeth saw the filthy, terrible place, she found her purpose. She became like an angel to the women there. She prayed for and with them, and she taught them to get along and to be fair to one another. When they wanted to set up a school in prison, Elizabeth helped make it happen.

Helping women in prison led Elizabeth into a lifetime of making things better for the poor. She became well known, a celebrity. And because of that, she was able to get help from the queen and other leaders. Her mission grew throughout Europe. Prison life got better. Many were helped by her kindness.

Elizabeth was strong about her opinions. She never gave up. She stood up to those who were against her, and she got things done. Are you like her? What have you done to help others?

THE LORD GOD. . .HAS APPOINTED ME TO TELL THE GOOD NEWS TO THE POOR.
HE HAS SENT ME TO COMFORT THOSE WHOSE HEARTS ARE BROKEN.
Isaiah 61:1 NCV

RUTH BELL GRAHAM
(1920–2007)

⋆⋆⋆⋆⋆⋆⋆⋆

A Love Story

As a teen, Ruth Bell already had her life planned. She would be a missionary to nomads in Tibet. (Nomads have no permanent home. They lead herds of farm animals to graze in fresh pastures.) Ruth's parents were missionaries in China, so she knew that being a missionary was hard work. Still, it's what she wanted to do.

Her plan changed when, in college, she met a handsome young preacher named Billy Graham. Ruth fell head over heels in love with him. He fell for her too! Billy was certain that God had planned for them to be together forever. She was "the one."

Billy had two life-changing questions for Ruth. First, "Will you marry me?" Then, "Will you give up your dream of being a missionary and help me grow my ministry?" He felt in his heart that it was the right thing for her to do.

Giving up her dream to move to Tibet wasn't an easy decision. Ruth prayed hard about it, and God led her to answer yes to both questions. The couple was married in 1943.

Ruth soon discovered that being a minister's wife was also hard work! But she was much more than Billy's wife. She worked behind the scenes to help him build a huge ministry that led, and continues to lead, hundreds of thousands of people to accept Jesus into their hearts. She and Billy became the perfect team. Where he was weak, she was strong. Together they reached many more for Christ than Ruth would have if she had gone to Tibet.

Ruth and Billy's love story ended when Ruth died sixty-four years after they were married. Although they were apart, Billy continued to love her. He was sure they would be together again in heaven.

What is true love? Read 1 Corinthians 13:4–7.

. . . .

LOVE EACH OTHER WITH GENUINE AFFECTION, AND TAKE DELIGHT IN HONORING EACH OTHER.
ROMANS 12:10 NLT

Betty Greene
(1920–97)

Adventuresome Pilot

In 1927 Charles Lindbergh became the first pilot to fly across the Atlantic Ocean. Americans watched when his plane left New York. They celebrated when it landed in Paris. Later eight-year-old Betty Greene saw Lindbergh in person, and she decided she wanted to be a pilot and have adventures too.

Betty received the best gift ever on her sixteenth birthday—flying lessons. Her dream to pilot a plane came true, and oh how she loved to fly! She wanted to work as a pilot, but in those days piloting a plane wasn't a common job for women. Her parents encouraged Betty to be a nurse, but that idea didn't interest her.

She followed her dream. Her first job was flying for the American military. Betty flew test missions, especially testing planes at high altitudes. The dangerous work didn't scare her. Maybe she felt closer to God up in the sky.

Betty's Christian faith led her to the next step in her flying career. She and three other pilots started an aviation ministry. Their idea was to serve missionaries in other countries. Betty became the Mission Aviation Fellowship's first pilot when she set out to fly missionaries from California to Mexico City. Her work took her to remote areas in the Amazon region, Sudan, Nigeria, Indonesia—thirty-two countries in all. She transported missionaries to their camps, brought them medical supplies and food, and flew sick and injured people to hospitals. For sixteen years, Betty flew missions for the Lord. What had once seemed her impossible dream had become reality.

Betty's story reminds us that nothing is impossible for God. He took her dream and worked it into an amazing way to serve Him. The Mission Aviation Fellowship Betty started continues today with 135 airplanes serving missionaries around the world.

"BUT WITH GOD EVERYTHING IS POSSIBLE."
MATTHEW 19:26 NLT

LADY JANE GREY
(1537–54)

The Nine-Day Queen

In medieval England, a few kings and queens came to rule in sneaky ways. Jane was one of them. Her story is about how what others wanted led to her becoming queen—*and* also to her death! It happened at a time when Protestants and Catholics disagreed so strongly about their beliefs that some were murdered.

Jane was born into a royal family. When she was old enough, Jane's dad arranged her marriage to a duke named John Dudley. Jane's cousin Edward would become King Edward VI. He had a half sister named Mary. All this is important because Jane, her dad, John, and Edward were Protestant. Edward's sister, Mary, was Catholic.

Edward was just ten when he became king. A sickly boy, by the time he reached fifteen Edward lay dying. Mary was next in line to rule, but neither Edward nor Jane's husband, John, wanted a Catholic queen. So John convinced Edward to make Jane queen instead. Jane hadn't been told, and she was not happy with their plan. But when Edward died, she took the throne.

Her reign didn't last long. Mary was furious. That crown belonged to her! She managed to convince others in power that she should be queen, and just nine days after Jane was crowned, Mary kicked her out.

Queen Mary and Jane's family strongly disagreed over whose religious beliefs were right. When Jane spoke out against what the queen believed, Mary ordered her execution.

As Jane waited in the tower cell knowing she would die, she refused to deny her beliefs. Just before she was beheaded, Jane quoted Jesus' words from the cross: "Father, into Your hands I give My spirit" (Luke 23:46). Those were her last words.

If you had been Jane, would you have denied your beliefs to save your life?

. . . .

"IF ANYONE WANTS TO KEEP HIS LIFE SAFE, HE WILL LOSE IT.
IF ANYONE GIVES UP HIS LIFE BECAUSE OF ME, HE WILL SAVE IT."
MATTHEW 16:25

Bethany Hamilton-Dirks
(1990–)

❧✦❧

Shark Attack

Roadblocks pop up in life, forcing us to find ways past them or to turn around and go back. On October 31, 2003, Bethany Hamilton faced the biggest roadblock of her life. She had no choice. She had to get past it.

Thirteen-year-old Bethany went surfing that morning with her dad and her best friend. Bethany loved surfing, and she was good at it. She lived in Hawaii where almost everyone surfed. By the time she was eight, Bethany did competitive surfing. But on that morning, she surfed just for fun. She lay on her surfboard, arms dangling in the water, waiting for a wave.

Suddenly, Bethany felt pressure on her left arm, then a jolt that joggled her arm a few times. The water around her turned red. Her left arm was missing, bitten off at the shoulder by a shark!

Everything happened quickly then. Bethany remembers the paramedic saying to her on the ride to the hospital, "God will never leave you or forsake you." His words were true. Bethany believed them. She believed in God, and she trusted Him to get her through the next days, weeks, months—years? She didn't know how long she had to live. Bethany had lost almost 60 percent of her blood. But whatever happened, God was with her.

Bethany lived, and she was determined not to allow the loss of an arm to keep her from surfing. One month after the attack, she was back on her surfboard, and she was still an awesome surfer, so awesome that she won competitions—and she continues to win. Today Bethany is a wife and mom. She surfs and gives speeches about surfing, the shark attack, and God.

When you face a roadblock, remember that God is with you. Trust Him to help.

"Be strong and have strength of heart! Do not be afraid or lose faith.
For the Lord your God is with you anywhere you go."
Joshua 1:9

HANNAH
(1 SAMUEL 1:1–2:1, 21)

✧~✦✦✦~✧

Hannah and the Bully

The Bible is filled with little stories like Hannah's. Read closely, or you might miss them.

Hannah and Peninnah were Elkanah's wives. (Back then men often had more than one.) Peninnah enjoyed bullying Hannah because Peninnah had children and Hannah didn't. The bullying made Hannah very sad, but instead of talking back and making the situation even worse, Hannah took her trouble to God.

She went to the temple and prayed, asking God for a son. Hannah promised that if God gave her a son, she would give the boy back to Him. She would allow him to be raised in the temple so he would grow up to serve God.

The head priest, Eli, saw Hannah crying and praying. He wondered what troubled her that made her so sad. Hannah told him that she was troubled and how much she wanted children. Eli prayed for her and said, "Go in peace. May the God of Israel do what you have asked of Him" (1 Samuel 1:17).

Then Hannah felt better. She wasn't as sad anymore.

God answered Hannah's prayer! He gave her a son. She named him Samuel, which means "asked of God." And Hannah kept her promise. When Samuel was old enough, she took him to the temple and asked Eli the priest to raise him and teach him to serve God. Can you imagine how hard that must have been? But Hannah trusted God and believed that Samuel would grow up to do great things. And he did. Samuel became a priest, judge, and prophet—a person who speaks for God.

God blessed Hannah with five more children. And Peninnah? The Bible says nothing more about the bully.

If someone hurts your feelings, be like Hannah. Tell God. He loves you. He will help take away your sadness.

• •

LORD, EVEN WHEN I HAVE TROUBLE ALL AROUND ME, YOU WILL KEEP ME ALIVE.
WHEN MY ENEMIES ARE ANGRY, YOU WILL REACH DOWN AND SAVE ME BY YOUR POWER.
PSALM 138:7 NCV

Marion Harvey
(1660–80)

❧⟡⟐⟡❧

Rebel for Freedom

Marion Harvey's parents raised her in a Christian Protestant home. Still, Marion didn't want Jesus in her heart. She rebelled in her teens and did things God says are sinful. Then one day she happened to hear ministers in the fields preaching about Jesus. They were rebels too, but in a good way.

Marion lived in Scotland in the 1600s when the government was Catholic and kings ruled that everyone else should be Catholic. The ministers in the fields rebelled against the king's rule and also over some things the Catholics believed. They wanted people to have freedom to disagree and follow their own beliefs.

When Marion heard the Bible preached and learned that Jesus is the only way to heaven, she welcomed Jesus into her heart. She turned away from doing bad things and did her best to obey God. Marion attended those outdoor worship services, and she learned about the Bible and Jesus from the ministers there. Her faith in God and love for Jesus grew strong.

On her way home from a service, the king's soldiers stopped her. They asked if she knew the men who preached there. They questioned whether Marion agreed with them. Marion stood up for what she believed. She answered yes to the soldiers' questions. Then they arrested Marion and put her in prison.

The king's men asked her many more questions. When Marion said Jesus Christ is head of the Church, the king's men had heard enough. The government sentenced her to die by hanging. She was just twenty years old.

Marion is one of many men and women throughout history who have given their lives for what they believed.

Do you think Marion was right to rebel against the king's law? Should people have freedom to disagree and follow their own beliefs?

....

CHRIST MADE US FREE. STAY THAT WAY. DO NOT GET CHAINED
ALL OVER AGAIN IN THE LAW AND ITS KIND OF RELIGIOUS WORSHIP.

GALATIANS 5:1

HULDAH
(2 KINGS 22:14-20; 2 CHRONICLES 34:22-33)

The Prophetess

Huldah's is another small story in the Bible. Not much is written about her, but what she did was life changing.

We know that she lived during the reign of Judah's King Josiah, a good king who loved God. He became king following years—generations—of bad kings. Josiah was eight when he took the throne and eighteen when he discovered something great.

While his men worked on making changes to the temple, they found a scroll, "The Book of the Law." This scroll held God's laws given to Moses many years before. The bad kings had hidden it! When Josiah read the laws, he discovered how disobedient the Jews had been. They had worshipped false gods and done many other things of which God did not approve.

Huldah, wife of the king's wardrobe keeper, was a prophetess—a woman with the gift of talking with God and passing His words to the people. Josiah sent his men to her to ask what God had to say to the people. Josiah knew Israel had disobeyed God's law.

Huldah said God was angry with His people for the things they had done. The Book of the Law said God would punish His people for disobeying. But when Huldah talked with God, He told her He was pleased with Josiah. He promised to hold off His punishment as long as Josiah lived.

The king's men carried God's message back to the king, and Josiah believed what Huldah said. For the rest of his life, Josiah took away the false gods and led the Israelites to worship God the right way. As long as he lived, the people followed the Law and there was peace.

Today God speaks to us through the Bible. Read it and listen to your heart. What is God telling you?

"CALL TO ME, AND I WILL ANSWER YOU. AND I WILL SHOW YOU GREAT AND WONDERFUL THINGS WHICH YOU DO NOT KNOW."
JEREMIAH 33:3

ANNE HUTCHINSON
(1591–1643)

Pioneer of Women's Rights

Anne Marbury grew up in England during the time when the Church of England ruled and the Puritans rebelled. Her parents taught her to think for herself instead of following the crowd. This was especially important in matters of religion. Her dad disagreed with what the church taught, and he encouraged Anne to question their beliefs too.

When Anne was older, she married William Hutchinson. The couple enjoyed listening to a Puritan minister, John Cotton. The Church of England disliked John for his teachings, so John moved across the ocean to the Massachusetts Bay Colony in America. Anne and William followed him. They thought that everyone in the colony would have complete freedom to believe and worship as they pleased. That wasn't what happened.

The colony's governor, John Winthrop, wanted everyone to follow strict Puritan rules. That meant women were to keep their beliefs to themselves and allow the men to lead.

But Anne wasn't going to keep quiet! She held meetings in her house where people could discuss religion. The number of people attending her meetings grew. Many began questioning the beliefs of the Puritan Church of Boston, and that upset Governor Winthrop—a lot!

He claimed it wasn't right for a woman to teach men, and he put Anne on trial for heresy—which meant teaching something that was against what the church believed. At her trial, Anne challenged the beliefs of the Boston church. She answered the governor's questions by quoting Bible verses. Winthrop found Anne's answers disrespectful. The rulers found Anne guilty and kicked her out of the colony!

Anne Hutchinson was one of the few Puritan women courageous enough to speak up.

Think about it: it was women like Anne who gave women in America courage to continue speaking up and fighting for what they believe.

OPEN YOUR MOUTH FOR THOSE WHO CANNOT SPEAK,
AND FOR THE RIGHTS OF THOSE WHO ARE LEFT WITHOUT HELP.
PROVERBS 31:8

Jairus's Daughter
(Matthew 9:18–25; Mark 5:21–43; Luke 8:41–56)

"Little Girl, Get Up!"

Who was Jairus's daughter? The Bible doesn't say much about her, not even her name, only that she was twelve years old and very sick. Her dad, Jairus, worried she might die. But he believed there was still hope in Jesus. He trusted that Jesus could heal his daughter, if only he could get to Him and ask.

Wherever Jesus went, crowds followed. A sea of people stood between Jairus and Jesus. He pushed his way through. Finally, he reached Jesus and said, "My little daughter is almost dead. Will You come so she may be healed and live?" Jairus knew time was running out for his girl.

Jesus went with Jairus, and so did the crowd. Everyone wanted to see what Jesus would do. They were almost to Jairus's house when Jesus suddenly stopped. "Who touched me?" He asked.

A woman who needed healing had pushed through the crowd to Jesus and touched His robe. While Jesus talked with her and healed her, some of Jairus's friends arrived with sad news. Time had run out. His little girl had died!

Can you imagine how Jairus felt? If only the crowd hadn't gotten in his way; if only Jesus hadn't stopped to heal that woman, Jairus's daughter might have lived.

"Jairus," Jesus said, "do not be afraid. Only believe." Then Jesus went with Jairus into his house. He ordered the crowd to stay outside. Jesus held the dead girl's hand and told her, "Little girl, get up!" She opened her eyes, and she was well!

From her story, we learn about patience. Often we want God to give us what we want right away. As impatient as you might feel for God to work in your life, it's important to keep on praying, trusting, and believing He will help you.

BE HAPPY IN YOUR HOPE. DO NOT GIVE UP WHEN TROUBLE COMES. DO NOT LET ANYTHING STOP YOU FROM PRAYING.
ROMANS 12:12

JOCHEBED
(EXODUS 2:1-10)

Baby in a Basket

Jochebed's story is about a time when Egypt's pharaoh ruled over God's people, the Israelites. Jochebed, an Israelite, had just given birth to a beautiful baby boy. A baby is something to be happy about, but Jochebed was also afraid.

The pharaoh, who was not a nice king, thought the Israelites might become powerful enough to overthrow his government. Each boy baby meant more men to fight in the future. So Pharaoh ruled that all Israelite boy babies be killed!

Of course Jochebed was afraid! She hid her baby for three months, but as the baby got older, Jochebed knew she couldn't hide him forever. She created a basket for him made from straw and tar. Then she put him in the basket and set it in tall grass next to the Nile River. She hoped someone would find him and save his life.

Jochebed's older daughter Miriam hid near the river and watched to see what would happen to her baby brother.

Just then Pharaoh's daughter and her servants arrived! They heard the baby cry. Pharaoh's daughter went to him and felt sorry for him. "He's an Israelite," she said.

Miriam came out from hiding with a plan. "If you want to keep him, I'll find an Israelite woman to raise him until he's older," she said.

Pharaoh's daughter agreed.

Who did Miriam come back with? Her mother! Jochebed raised her son until he wasn't a baby anymore. Then she gave him back to Pharaoh's daughter.

That baby boy grew up to be Moses, the man who led the Israelites out of Egypt and freed them from the pharaoh's rules.

Letting go of something you love is always hard. But you can trust that when you have to let go, God is right there. He has a plan—a good one.

"FOR MY THOUGHTS ARE NOT YOUR THOUGHTS, AND MY WAYS ARE NOT YOUR WAYS," SAYS THE LORD.
ISAIAH 55:8

ESTHER JOHN
(1929–60)

Secret Admirer

In 1929 a Muslim family in South India welcomed their new baby into the world. They named her Qumar Zia.

Qumar attended government schools in India. Then she moved to a Christian school. She felt amazed when her teacher talked openly about Jesus. Everything Qumar learned about Him was new. She began reading the Bible, and one day while reading the book of Isaiah, Qumar welcomed Jesus into her heart. She kept it a secret. Her family wouldn't approve if they knew Qumar loved Jesus and read the Bible. She read it secretly at night with a flashlight under the covers.

When Qumar was older, her dad arranged for her to marry a Muslim man. Qumar didn't want to, so she ran away from home. She went to Pakistan and changed her name to Esther John. She believed God was leading her to go into the small villages and tell the field workers about Jesus.

Esther moved in with an American missionary couple, the Whites. She often rode her bike to nearby villages where she taught women to read. She told them about Jesus and that He came to save us from sin.

For the rest of her life, Esther brought the Good News about Jesus to the people in the fields. She never returned home to her parents, because when Esther was just thirty years old, the Whites found her dead in her room.

The people in those little villages never forgot about Esther. The story of her strong Christian faith spread around the world. Today there is even a statue of her at Westminster Abbey, in London.

How do you think Esther felt when she learned about Jesus? Why do you think she felt it was important to share the Good News with others?

[JESUS] SAID TO THEM, "YOU ARE TO GO TO ALL THE WORLD AND PREACH THE GOOD NEWS TO EVERY PERSON."
MARK 16:15

ANN JUDSON
(1789–1826)

Faraway Lands

Ann was a teenager when she accepted Jesus into her heart. She studied the Bible and talked with God in prayer. She wanted God to use her. Ann asked Him to lead her where He wanted her to go.

God heard. He already had a plan for her to be a missionary on the other side of the world. Ann wouldn't be one of *many* American women missionaries overseas—she would be the first!

A young minister named Adoniram Judson was key to God's plan. He wanted to be a missionary overseas too. When he met Ann, Adoniram quickly learned that they shared that dream of faraway places. The two fell in love, got married, and sailed to India.

When the Judsons arrived in India, they weren't welcome. They went instead to Burma (today it is Myanmar), a country between India and China. God never makes mistakes. He knew what He was doing. The 15 million people of Burma hadn't heard about Jesus. Now God had Ann and Adoniram exactly where He wanted them.

Burma became their home. The Burmese people accepted that Ann and Adoniram loved Jesus, but they didn't want Him. Ann found it hard to find words in their language to explain that Jesus came so they might live forever in heaven. Still, she tried. Ann translated the Gospel into their language. Slowly, the people began accepting Jesus.

Ann also wrote about her work in Burma. American women read her stories, and many more decided to become missionaries in faraway lands. That was the best part of God's plan. Because God sent Ann, today it's common for American women to serve Him as missionaries overseas.

Do you see how God worked out every detail of His plan? He knows exactly what to do, and everything He does is perfect.

He is like a rock; what He does is perfect, and He is always fair.
DEUTERONOMY 32:4 NCV

Mary Jane Kinnaird
(1816–88)

Generosity

Do you know a kid who lives with someone other than their parents? Mary Jane's parents died when she was little. Her grandpa, older brother, and aunts and uncles raised her. Mary Jane's family was blessed with money, so she had a governess too.

Bible study was important to Mary Jane. Her uncle was a minister where they lived in England, and when Mary Jane was older, she became his secretary. At the same time, she began making plans to help others. Surely her family had enough money to be generous. Mary Jane's first project was a training school for servants who worked doing chores like cooking, laundry, and cleaning for others.

She had lots of ideas! And Mary Jane made them happen after she married a wealthy man named Arthur Kinnaird. He liked being around people, and she enjoyed working behind the scenes. They made a great team. Together they raised money for many good causes.

But it was her first project, the training school for servants, that led to something wonderful. Mary Jane made it grow until it became four schools. Then she combined it with a Bible study group. The organization became the Young Women's Christian Association—the YWCA!

You've probably heard of it. Today the YWCA helps women and girls from all backgrounds become the best they can be. It promotes leadership and the idea that everyone is equal.

Mary Jane helped others with her money, but there are other ways to be generous. Can you name a few? Her story, along with the others in this book, reminds us that God doesn't care how you start out in life. He uses all kinds of people to help others, rich and poor, outgoing and shy, from all kinds of families.

GOD DOES NOT SHOW FAVORITISM.
Romans 2:11 NLT

ISOBEL KUHN
(1901–57)

Isobel and the Needle's Eye

Riches come in forms other than money. For some people, their stuff is their riches. For others, their free time is their treasure. Jesus said what we love on the earth is temporary. His promise of living forever in heaven is what truly makes a person rich. Someone gets that kind of rich by putting God first, making Him more important than anyone or anything else.

Isobel Kuhn took awhile to figure that out. A wild and rebellious teen, she turned against her parents' strong Christian beliefs. Isobel wasn't sure if God existed, and she didn't care until she became depressed after a breakup with her boyfriend. She prayed, "God, if there be a God, if You will prove to me that You are, and if You will give me peace, I will give You my whole life."

The change didn't happen overnight, but slowly Isobel accepted God's peace. She gave up what she thought made her rich and turned it over to Him. Isobel felt God leading her to mission work in China, so she packed her bags and went.

Life there wasn't easy. She faced all kinds of trouble, but with each obstacle she grew closer to God. The people she ministered to were very poor. Some had bugs in their homes, and if they visited Isobel in her house, their children made a mess. Those little things bothered Isobel. But finally she learned to put God first in everything. All that mattered then was Him, and Isobel sharing with others the Good News about Jesus.

Isobel's story is a reminder of something else Jesus said: "It is easier for a camel to go through the eye of a needle than for a rich man to go to heaven" (Mark 10:25). What do you think that means?

"WHOEVER DOES NOT GIVE UP ALL THAT HE HAS, CANNOT BE MY FOLLOWER."
LUKE 14:33

Jeanette Li
(1899–1968)

Stay Near to God

When Jeanette Li was a little girl in South China, her father, a Buddhist, worshipped idols instead of the one true God. Something in Jeanette's heart told her this was wrong. Her mother felt it too. Neither knew then about the real God and Jesus.

Jeanette heard about Jesus when she was seven and sick with a fever. At a missionary hospital, the doctors told her that God sent Jesus to die on the cross so everyone could be forgiven for their sins and live in heaven with Him forever. Jeanette wanted that kind of forgiveness. She prayed and asked Jesus into her heart. After that Jeanette attended a Christian school and was baptized at age ten. Her mother became a believer and was baptized too. Their new life in Christ was wonderful, but it came at a price. Their family disowned them because they had turned from the Buddhist religion. It hurt, but they believed that nothing, not even their family, could pull them away from God.

Sometimes without noticing, we carelessly drift away from God. That happened to Jeanette. She studied hard to become a teacher, and all that studying took her away from praying and reading the Bible. Thankfully, Jeanette noticed herself becoming distant from God, and she concentrated on staying near to Him.

God used Jeanette for the rest of her life to share the news about Jesus. Life was difficult sometimes, but whenever she needed something, God was there to help. In her autobiography, Jeanette wrote: "In every period of my life, I have found God sufficient for my every need, for my help in every weakness."

If you find yourself drifting, think of Jeanette and remember: stay close to God. Whatever you need, He will provide for you, just as He did for her.

"Ask, and what you are asking for will be given to you. Look, and what you are looking for you will find. Knock, and the door you are knocking on will be opened to you."
Matthew 7:7

LOIS
(2 TIMOTHY 1:5)

Grandma Lois

Many of the Bible's New Testament books are letters written by a Christian named Paul. He preached about Jesus to anyone who would listen. Paul stayed true to Jesus even when unbelievers beat him and threw him into jail.

While in jail, Paul spent his time writing letters encouraging his friends to stay strong in their faith. You will find Lois's name only once in the Bible, in a letter Paul wrote to his friend Timothy. Paul was like a father to Timothy. He shared wise advice with this younger Christian friend, and in his letter Paul also wrote about Timothy's faith. He said, "I remember your true faith. It is the same faith your grandmother Lois had and your mother Eunice had" (2 Timothy 1:5).

From Paul's words, we know that Lois was Timothy's grandmother and that she had "true faith." She taught Timothy to have that kind of faith too. That's all the Bible tells us about Lois. She was probably like many grandmothers today who love their children, grandchildren—and Jesus!

A Lois kind of grandma is an older woman who believes without doubting that Jesus is the only way to heaven. She trusts Jesus as Savior and loves Him because He loves us. And when her faith is tested, a Lois kind of grandma stays strong. Nothing can stop her from trusting God! She wants her children and grandchildren to have true faith too. So she teaches them about Jesus and leads them to trust Him.

Christian grandmas are often very wise. They've learned how to stay strong when their faith is tested. Maybe you know an older woman, like Timothy's Grandma Lois, who loves Jesus. What might you learn from her? Ask her to talk with you about true faith.

AND SO LET US COME NEAR TO GOD WITH A TRUE HEART FULL OF FAITH.
HEBREWS 10:22

Katharine von Bora Luther
(1499–1552)

"Dear Kate"

Imagine this: You are only three years old when your family sends you away to a convent school. You spend your childhood there, and when you are a teenager you do what your family expects from you. You take your vows and become a nun. You're not happy. You want to get out. But escaping from the convent is dangerous. If caught, you could spend your life in prison.

That's how Katharine von Bora's story begins in sixteenth-century Germany. It was the time when Protestants fought to break away from the Catholic Church. One of the most well-known Protestant leaders was Martin Luther. Katharine secretly contacted him and asked for his help.

Luther put together a plan. The night before Easter in 1523, Katharine escaped by hiding in an empty fish barrel on a merchant's wagon! She was taken to Luther, who didn't know what to do with her. It was a crime to hide her. Her family had disowned her. The only options left were marriage or the convent. Maybe he could find a husband for her? Those ideas failed, so Martin Luther married her himself.

They grew to love each other deeply. Luther called her his "Dear Kate." He knew she was smart. He gave her complete control of their household—unheard of back then—and he listened to her advice, something men of that era rarely did. Katharine stood by her man and helped as he led the Protestants to form a new church.

Katharine was a strong woman who, by example, encouraged other women to become strong in their marriages. She wasn't afraid to speak up and speak out for what she believed. She served her family well.

What do you think it means for a woman to serve her family? What makes her strong?

WHO CAN FIND A GOOD WIFE? FOR SHE IS WORTH FAR MORE THAN RUBIES THAT MAKE ONE RICH.
PROVERBS 31:10

LYDIA
(ACTS 16:12-15, 40)

✦❧∽⟩∽⟨❧✦

Europe's First Christian

Do you like the color purple? If you said yes, then you and Lydia have something in common. The Bible says that Lydia sold purple cloth. That doesn't tell us much about her, but when we think of Lydia living back in the first century, we can assume a few other things. She owned a business, something uncommon for women of her time. And she probably had money, because purple was the color worn by royalty, and the rich bought her cloth.

Lydia lived in Philippi, a large and important city in Macedonia (today it is Greece) ruled by the Romans. In a dream, Jesus' follower Paul heard a man tell him to travel to Philippi and share the Good News about Jesus. So Paul went and took along his friend Timothy.

Some people in Philippi believed in the one true God, but they hadn't heard about Jesus. Lydia was one of them. One day she went with some women to a peaceful area near a river to pray. There she met Timothy and Paul. She listened as Paul talked about Jesus being the only way to heaven. Lydia believed his words, and she invited Jesus into her heart.

Lydia became the first person in Europe to become a Christian! But her story doesn't end there. She invited Paul and Timothy to stay at her house. She asked many times. She insisted! So they went, and they told her more about Jesus. Then Lydia told others and helped to spread the Good News. While Paul was in Philippi, he and his friends were always welcome in her home.

Think about it. What if Paul hadn't gone to Philippi? Do you believe the Good News would have spread beyond the Jewish people, throughout Europe and the world?

• •

LET ME TELL YOU THAT THE GOOD NEWS IS FOR THE PEOPLE WHO ARE NOT JEWS ALSO. THEY ARE ABLE TO HAVE LIFE THAT LASTS FOREVER. . .THEY ARE TO RECEIVE ALL THAT GOD HAS PROMISED THROUGH CHRIST.
EPHESIANS 3:6

Catherine Marshall
(1914–83)

Christian Author

God often brings people together in the present as part of His future plan. For example, on the day your mom and dad met, they didn't know you would be a part of their future. But here you are! God already knew that you would be their child. God knows everything about you. He already has a plan for your life.

When Catherine Wood attended college in Georgia, she met a young Scottish preacher named Peter Marshall. The two got married, and Catherine settled into life as a preacher's wife. Before long Peter was asked to pastor a church in Washington, DC.

Catherine had no idea how famous her husband would become. People loved his sermons. The US Senate asked Peter to be their chaplain, and he served there until he died of a heart attack at the young age of forty-six.

When Peter died, Catherine became a single mom raising their nine-year-old son. She felt close to Peter when she read notes and diaries she had written during her time with him. Catherine wanted to keep his memory alive, so she published a book of Peter's best sermons. It instantly became a bestseller.

That book was the first of many Catherine wrote. For the rest of her life, she penned bestselling nonfiction books, biographies, and novels for adults, children, and teens. One of her books, *A Man Called Peter*, was made into a movie. Her book *Christy* became a television series.

When Catherine met Peter, she didn't know that marrying him would lead to her becoming one of the most famous Christian authors of all time. But all along that was God's plan.

Only God knows what He has planned for you. Do you wonder who you will meet? Are you excited to see where God will lead you?

ALL THE DAYS PLANNED FOR ME WERE WRITTEN IN YOUR BOOK BEFORE I WAS ONE DAY OLD.
PSALM 139:16 NCV

Martha
(LUKe 10:38–42)

Company Is Coming!

When company comes to your house, how do you prepare? You do everything you can think of to make your guests feel welcome. You put your whole heart into entertaining them by going out of your way to be warm, generous, and kind. Making company feel welcome is called hospitality, and it's a good thing.

What if your guest was Jesus?

Mary and Martha were grown-up sisters and Jesus' close friends. They lived together, and whenever Jesus and His disciples came to their village, Jesus stayed with them.

Martha was all about hospitality. Imagine how concerned she became when Jesus arrived in their village. She had no warning. There were no smartphones or computers back then. Jesus couldn't call or text to say He was coming. He just showed up. And when He did, Martha got busy.

When Jesus arrived, Martha was making supper. She and Mary welcomed their friend in. While Martha went back to preparing a nice meal, Mary sat by Jesus and listened to everything He said.

That upset Martha. There she was working hard, and Mary was doing nothing! Martha came to Jesus and said, "Do You see that my sister is not helping me? Tell her to help me."

Jesus answered, "Martha, Martha, you are worried and troubled about many things. Only a few things are important, even just one. Mary has chosen the good thing. It will not be taken away from her" (Luke 10:40–42).

Martha's story reminds us that Jesus should be our first priority. Everything He says is important. If you get too busy to spend time with Him every day by praying and reading His words in your Bible, stop and remember Martha. Make the time you spend with Jesus more important than anything else.

....

"DON'T WOrrY AND SAY, 'WHAT WILL WE EAT?' Or 'WHAT WILL WE DRINK?' Or 'WHAT WILL WE WEAR?' . . .
SEEK FIRST GOD'S KINGDOM AND WHAT GOD WANTS. THEN ALL YOUR OTHER NEEDS WILL BE MET AS WELL."
MATTHEW 6:31, 33 NCV

MARY, MOTHER OF JESUS
(LUKE 1:26–38)

Steadfast Trust

Even those who don't read the Bible know this Mary's story. It's a lesson about trusting God when you don't understand why He has led you into an unbelievable situation.

Mary was a young woman planning her wedding. She and her fiancé, Joseph, made promises to each other—one of them that they wouldn't have a baby until after they married. Until then they would live like a brother and sister.

Mary learned about God's plan on a day that began like any other. She was going about her work when God's angel, Gabriel, appeared from nowhere. "Greetings!" he said. "The Lord has blessed you and is with you" (Luke 1:28).

Mary was very afraid.

The angel said, "Don't be afraid, Mary; God has shown you his grace. Listen! You will become pregnant and give birth to a son, and you will name him Jesus. He will be great and will be called the Son of the Most High. . . . He will rule over the people. . .forever, and his kingdom will never end" (Luke 1:30–33 NCV).

"But how can this happen?" Mary asked. "Joseph and I aren't married."

"God can do anything!" said the angel (Luke 1:37 NCV). He explained that God's Spirit would mysteriously put the baby inside Mary. God would be the baby's Father.

Can you imagine trusting an angel from God who told you something so beyond belief? But Mary did. She trusted God even when His purpose was unclear. "I am the servant of the Lord," she told the angel. "Let this happen to me as you say!" (Luke 1:38 NCV).

Maybe that's why God chose this Mary as Jesus' mom—because her trust was so great.

Take a minute to examine your trust in God. Is it strong like Mary's?

. . . .

THE LORD IS MY LIGHT AND THE ONE WHO SAVES ME. WHOM SHOULD I FEAR?
THE LORD IS THE STRENGTH OF MY LIFE. OF WHOM SHOULD I BE AFRAID?
PSALM 27:1

MARY MAGDALENE
(Mark 16:9; Luke 8:2; John 20:1–18)

Grateful Mary

Do you have more than one friend with the same first name? Maybe you know two Emmas or two Ethans. How do you describe them so others will know which friend you mean? "Emma who lives down the street." "Ethan, Sophia's brother." Do you use their last names?

There are six Marys in the Bible. Three of them are well known in stories about Jesus. They are Mary, Jesus' mother; Mary from the village of Bethany; and Mary Magdalene from a place called Magdala near the Sea of Galilee.

If you had known Mary Magdalene, you might have called her "Grateful Mary." Her story begins in a terrible way. The Bible says she was possessed by seven demons, and Jesus cast them out (Mark 16:9; Luke 8:2). You can only imagine what those "demons" were, but they made her sick. Mary's life was awful. Jesus made her better, and she was grateful. We know Mary loved Jesus, because she became one of His followers.

Her story continues on the day Jesus died on the cross. Mary was there. How sad she must have felt seeing Him suffering. How terrible when He died. His friends put Jesus' body into a cavelike tomb and sealed it with a rock.

Three days later, Mary went to the tomb and found the rock moved away. Jesus' body was gone. "Where have they put Him?" she asked, crying. Then Mary turned and saw Jesus standing there alive. "Teacher!" Oh how grateful she was to see Him. He had come back, just as He promised His followers He would.

Jesus told Mary Magdalene to spread the Good News, and she became known as the first person ever to tell others, "He lives!"

How did you feel the first time you heard the Good News?

GOD RAISED JESUS FROM THE DEAD, AND IF GOD'S SPIRIT IS LIVING IN YOU,
HE WILL ALSO GIVE LIFE TO YOUR BODIES THAT DIE.
ROMANS 8:11 NCV

MARY OF BETHANY
(JOHN 11:1-44)

When Jesus Cried

Mary, Martha, and their brother, Lazarus, were Jesus' close friends. Whenever Jesus came to Bethany, He stayed with them. They knew each other well, and the three siblings trusted Jesus.

One day Lazarus became ill. His sisters worried that he might die, so they sent someone to find Jesus. They were sure that Jesus would heal their brother.

When Jesus heard, He decided to wait. He waited until He knew that Lazarus was dead, and then Jesus went to Bethany.

Martha ran to meet Him. "If You only had come right away, Lazarus would be alive," she said.

"He will rise and live again," said Jesus.

Martha thought Jesus meant Lazarus would live again in heaven.

"Martha, do you believe I am the Son of God?" Jesus asked.

"I do," she said.

Then Mary came with tears streaming down her face, her eyes swollen from crying. When Jesus saw how sad His friend was, He cried too. Jesus felt heartbroken to see her pain. But He had a good reason to wait until Lazarus died. Jesus was about to prove to disbelievers in Bethany that He truly was God's Son.

He went with the sisters to Lazarus's tomb. Many of the villagers came too. Then Jesus prayed, and in a loud voice He cried, "Lazarus, come out!"

Out came Lazarus, alive and perfectly well.

The villagers ran to tell others what Jesus did.

Why did Jesus cry when He saw Mary's tears? Jesus loved her. He didn't want her to feel sad. Still, He did what He knew was best to lead others to believe in Him.

Has someone you loved ever done something for your own good that made you cry? Do you think your tears made that person feel sad too?

"GOD WILL TAKE AWAY ALL THEIR TEARS. THERE WILL BE NO MORE DEATH OR SORROW OR CRYING OR PAIN."
REVELATION 21:4

Henrietta Mears
(1890–1963)

༺·৵৵৵ঌঌঌ·༻

Loving Teacher

How much time do you spend with your teachers? A lot!

A teacher's job is all about getting kids ready to be adults. It's more than teaching you to read, do math, and make exciting discoveries. A good teacher tries to understand you as a person and help you become the best you can be.

Henrietta Mears was that kind of teacher.

She loved God, and at age five she welcomed Jesus into her heart. Henrietta taught her first Sunday school class when she was twelve. She enjoyed teaching, and she was good at it. Henrietta decided to attend college and learn to become an even better teacher. While she was there learning, Henrietta noticed all the kids and grown-ups who hadn't yet asked Jesus into their hearts. So, as busy as she was with her own schoolwork, Henrietta still found time to teach Sunday school.

After graduating from college, Henrietta taught high school students. She loved "her kids," and she wanted to do more than teach them. Henrietta wanted to find out what was in their hearts. She wanted to know each child as an individual, so Henrietta created and participated in fun school activities like plays, fundraisers, and special projects to know her students better. She even started a football team! And, whenever she could, Henrietta led kids to Jesus.

Although she loved teaching high school, Henrietta felt God telling her to move on. She joined the ministry at the First Presbyterian Church of Hollywood, California. It was her job to improve the Sunday school there and to teach others to be Sunday school teachers. Henrietta was so good at her job that thousands of kids and grown-ups came to learn about Jesus.

Do you have a favorite teacher? How has that teacher helped you to be a better person?

. . . .

Bring up a child by teaching him the way he should go,
and when he is old he will not turn away from it.
Proverbs 22:6

Miriam
(EXODUS 2; 15:20–21; NUMBERS 12)

Siblings Behaving Badly

When Egypt's pharaoh decided the Israelites were becoming too powerful, he ordered his men to kill all the Jewish baby boys. Miriam saved her baby brother's life. She helped find a way to keep Moses alive. Because of her, Moses grew up to be a great leader of the Israelites.

Miriam and Moses also had a brother named Aaron. The three siblings were close to God. When God told Moses to lead the Israelites out of slavery in Pharaoh's Egypt, Moses, Miriam, and Aaron went together, leading God's people. With Pharaoh's soldiers chasing them, God split the Red Sea wide open, making a dry path for the Israelites to cross on. Then He closed it up, trapping Pharaoh's army. When they were safe on the other side, Miriam led the women in worshipping and thanking God (Exodus 15:20–21).

Escaping from Egypt was the beginning of a long, hard journey for the Israelites. For forty years, they wandered, waiting to enter the special land God had promised them.

God chose Moses to lead His people. That made Aaron and Miriam jealous. He was the baby of the family, after all! Why hadn't God also put His trust in them?

They complained about Moses, and when God heard, He came down in a cloud. He stood at the door of their tent and ordered them to come out. "Now, listen to Me," God said. Then He made it clear that He was angry with them for speaking against their brother. Miriam must have said really bad things about Moses, because God gave her a weeklong "time out."

Miriam's story reminds us to support and love our brothers and sisters all the time. If you feel angry or jealous toward your brother or sister, talk with God about it, and ask for His help.

BROTHERS AND SISTERS, DO NOT COMPLAIN AGAINST EACH OTHER
OR YOU WILL BE JUDGED GUILTY. AND THE JUDGE IS READY TO COME!
JAMES 5:9 NCV

LOTTIE MOON
(1840–1912)

Little Cookie Lady

Imagine using a yardstick to measure someone's height. A yardstick is thirty-six inches (three feet) long. Now add twelve inches. That's about how tall Lottie Moon was. As an adult, she stood just over four feet tall. But being little didn't stop her from reaching the big plans God had for her.

Lottie grew up in Virginia. Her parents were wealthy plantation owners and also Southern Baptists. Lottie's mom made sure Lottie knew about Jesus, but Lottie didn't care. She often felt unsure about what she wanted to do. Even when she decided to go to college, Lottie went to several schools before she settled on one and became serious about her studies and also about Jesus. She finally welcomed Him into her heart after she heard ministers speak at her school.

She loved Jesus and wanted to work in China as a missionary, but it was unusual then for unmarried women to serve as missionaries overseas. Still, God made it possible for Lottie to go.

In China, where few people believed in Jesus, Lottie found it difficult to encourage them to accept Christ as their Savior. She discovered that first she needed to be their friend and show them, instead of tell them, how to be Christians. She moved to a small village in the Chinese countryside and tried to be friendly with people there. Often she baked cookies. When children smelled the delicious treats baking, they went to her house, and before long Lottie met their mothers. As she made friends, the people began listening to her stories about Jesus, and many accepted Him into their hearts.

Maybe you know people who need Jesus. You're not too young or too small to make a difference. Be like Lottie. Set a good example. Ask God to help you lead them to Christ.

FOLLOW MY EXAMPLE, AS I FOLLOW THE EXAMPLE OF CHRIST.
1 CORINTHIANS 11:1 NCV

Naaman's Servant Girl
(2 Kings 5)

❧❧❧❧❧

All-Powerful God

Everyone has trouble sometimes. It doesn't matter who you are. Even the most powerful leaders become sick or have other problems. Jesus knew it! He told His followers, "In the world you will have much trouble. But take hope! I have power over the world!" (John 16:33).

In Bible times, Naaman, a leader of the Syrian army, had an awful skin disease. Could anyone heal him?

Syrian soldiers had raided a home and kidnapped a young Jewish girl. She became a servant slave to Naaman's wife. The Bible doesn't share her name, but we know she loved God and also that she trusted Elisha, one of God's prophets in Israel. When the girl saw how miserable Naaman was, she told his wife, "I wish that my owner's husband were with the man of God who is in Samaria! Then he would heal his bad skin disease" (2 Kings 5:3).

Naaman didn't believe in the one true God, but he was ready to try anything.

The sounds of Naaman's horses and wagons came near Elisha's house. When they stopped, Naaman went to Elisha's door. But Elisha didn't come out. Instead, he sent a man who told Naaman to wash seven times in the dirty Jordan River.

What? No way! Naaman expected Elisha to wave his hand and heal the disease. He felt angry and ready to leave, but his servants convinced him to do what Elisha said. So Naaman washed in the river, and he was healed! He understood then the power of the one and only God. From that day on, Naaman became a believer—thanks to a servant girl who bravely shared her trust in God's power.

If someone you know has trouble, be like the servant girl and help that person stay strong. Remind them that God can do anything.

• •

A Final Word: Be strong in the Lord and in His mighty power.
Ephesians 6:10 nlt

NAOMI
(RUTH 1-4)

Things Work Together for Good

Naomi's story begins with her feeling alone. Many years earlier, there was a famine in Bethlehem, where Naomi lived with her husband and their two sons. To find food, the family moved to Moab, a place about fifty miles away. Life there was good. They had food to eat, the boys grew up and married women from Moab. . .but then trouble came. Naomi's husband died. Her sons died too. The only people left with Naomi were her sons' wives—her daughters-in-law, Orpah and Ruth.

"Who will care for me in my old age?" Naomi worried. Loneliness made her want to return home to Bethlehem.

Both Orpah and Ruth loved Naomi. They said they would move to Bethlehem to be with her. But Naomi told them to stay in Moab and go on with their lives. Orpah stayed, but Ruth insisted on going. No way would she allow her mother-in-law to be alone! They walked fifty miles back to Bethlehem, bringing with them only what they needed for the trip.

They arrived in Bethlehem at harvesttime. Ruth went to work gathering grain in a field belonging to a man named Boaz, a relative of Naomi's husband. He was a wealthy man of God. When Boaz learned that Ruth had given up her life in Moab to stay with Naomi, he acted extra kindly toward her. He thought she was special for giving up everything for her mother-in-law.

Meanwhile, Naomi noticed there was something good going on between Boaz and Ruth. She wanted them to get married. And that's exactly what happened. Boaz and Ruth fell in love, and Naomi had a home with them for the rest of her life.

Naomi's story reminds us not to worry. God can take a bad situation and work it into something good.

WE KNOW THAT GOD MAKES ALL THINGS WORK TOGETHER FOR THE GOOD
OF THOSE WHO LOVE HIM AND ARE CHOSEN TO BE A PART OF HIS PLAN.
ROMANS 8:28

FLORENCE NIGHTINGALE
(1820–1910)

The Lady with the Lamp

If you've been in a hospital, you know it's a very clean place. It's kept clean so germs don't spread and make sick people even sicker. You might thank Florence Nightingale for that. In the 1800s, she spent her life working to improve unsanitary conditions in hospitals and making sure patients were well cared for.

It's a wonder Florence became a nurse. Her parents were against it. She came from a wealthy English family, and a woman in her social class was expected to marry a rich man and settle down. But Florence felt God wanted her to be a nurse. So, although her parents disapproved, she enrolled in nursing school.

As a nurse, Florence felt disgusted by how unclean some hospitals were. She saw patients becoming sicker and dying from being in dirty surroundings, so Florence made it her mission to clean things up. Her bosses noticed, and so did others. She became well known.

In 1853 war broke out, and Britain's Secretary of War asked Florence to gather a team of nurses to tend to British soldiers in military hospitals.

The conditions there were beyond horrible. Bugs and rodents darted through the filthy halls among the patients. The nurses didn't have what they needed. Florence ordered that the place be cleaned up and supplies be brought in. Then she got busy caring for the men. She cared for them day and night, carrying a lantern with her through the halls at night. They called her the "Lady with the Lamp."

Florence continued fighting for sanitary conditions in hospitals and better patient care. She became famous for her work and is known today as someone who led the way for modern nursing.

What did you learn from Florence's story? What can you do to clean up your surroundings?

· ·

ALL THINGS SHOULD BE DONE IN THE RIGHT WAY, ONE AFTER THE OTHER.
1 CORINTHIANS 14:40

NOAH'S WIFE
(GENESIS 6:18; 7:7, 13; 8:16, 19)

What If God Said. . . ?

You know the story of Noah's ark (Genesis 6–8:19): God saw His earth filling up with sin. He wanted to make it clean and right again. So God spoke to His friend Noah, a good man. God told Noah to build a huge boat—an ark—and to load two of each kind of animal onto it. Then He told Noah and his family (his wife, three sons, and their wives) to get into the ark. God shut the door and sealed them inside. The rest is history. A big flood destroyed everything on earth. But Noah, his family, and the animals were safe and left to start life over again.

The Bible doesn't say much about Noah's wife, but we can picture her as a patient woman with much faith in God and also her husband. What must she have thought when Noah said, "Honey, I just talked with God. He's going to destroy everything on earth, but don't worry. He has a plan. I'm to build a really, really big boat. We're going to load two of every kind of animal onto it and food for them and us and our family. Then we're going to get on the boat, and God will save us from whatever He is going to do."

Is it surprising that Noah's wife believed him? No, because she trusted God. As crazy as the idea sounded, this woman of faith went along with the plan.

The Bible says, "A woman who respects the LORD should be praised" (Proverbs 31:30 NCV). Noah and His wife both respected God. They were sure He loved them and that His plan was good.

Is your faith in God strong like Mrs. Noah's faith? Do you trust in His plans for you?

WHAT CAN WE SAY ABOUT ALL THESE THINGS? SINCE GOD IS FOR US, WHO CAN BE AGAINST US?
ROMANS 8:31

BETTY OLSEN
(1934–69)

Woman in a War Zone

When Jesus hung dying on the cross, He said, "Father, forgive them. They do not know what they are doing" (Luke 23:34). Betty Olsen was a Christian. She knew those words, and she likely remembered them in her final hours on earth.

Betty wanted to be a missionary nurse. She went to nursing school. Then, in 1964, she received an assignment to serve in a missionary hospital in Vietnam.

The country was in the middle of a deadly war. Betty's family and friends worried about her going, but Betty felt at peace with her assignment. She decided that even if she didn't come back, as many soldiers hadn't, she was carrying out God's will for her. Betty believed Vietnam was where she should be.

Several years into her assignment, the enemy raided the military hospital. They captured Betty along with two others, Michael Benge and Henry Blood. The prisoners were treated horribly—put in cages, starved, beaten, and made to walk for miles. Only Benge survived. Later he told the story of Betty's bravery and selflessness.

He said Betty gave to other prisoners the little food she was given. When Henry became sick from pneumonia and died, Betty prayed at his graveside. Benge said it was Betty's spiritual strength that kept them going. She kept praying. As sick and miserable as Betty must have been, it was she who nursed Benge when he became ill and almost died. When Betty became weak from walking through the jungle and being abused by her captors, they kicked and dragged her. Finally, they poisoned Betty. She died and went to be with Jesus.

Michael Benge said, "She never showed any bitterness or resentment. To the end, she loved the ones who mistreated her."

From Betty's story we learn the true meaning of courage and forgiveness.

. . . .

"BLESS THOSE WHO CURSE YOU, PRAY FOR THOSE WHO ARE CRUEL TO YOU."
LUKE 6:28 NCV

Rosa Parks
(1913–2005)

First Lady of Civil Rights

In the mid-1950s in Montgomery, Alabama, where Rosa Parks lived, many laws separated African-Americans from white people. These laws gave white people privileges that African-Americans didn't have. The same was true throughout much of the southern part of the United States. This was wrong. Many knew it, but Rosa Parks did something about it.

Buses had assigned seats, meaning that white people sat in the front half of the bus, and African-Americans in the back. A sign in the aisle separated the races.

One day Rosa sat near the middle of the bus in one of the first rows assigned to African-Americans. The bus filled with passengers, mostly white. All seats in the white section were taken, and a white man stood in the aisle. The bus driver told the African-Americans in their front rows to stand up and move back so the white passenger could sit. Rosa refused. She'd spent her life being told she wasn't good enough to sit in the front of the bus and do other things white people did, so Rosa said, "No." The driver called the police, and they arrested Rosa.

The African-American community in Montgomery decided to boycott the buses—that meant they wouldn't ride on them. They walked, rode bicycles, and found other transportation. They also got African-American leaders like Martin Luther King Jr. involved in working to change the law. The boycott lasted almost a year, and it was a huge success. The law changed so everyone could sit anywhere on buses. Today we celebrate what Rosa did and also that African-Americans have fought and won the right to be treated equally in every way to everyone else.

God created us to be equal. We are all the same in His sight, and that is how He wants us to treat each other.

IN CHRIST, THERE IS NO DIFFERENCE BETWEEN JEW AND GREEK, SLAVE AND FREE PERSON, MALE AND FEMALE. YOU ARE ALL THE SAME IN CHRIST JESUS.
GALATIANS 3:28 NCV

Perpetua

(?–203)

All for Jesus

Jesus said, "If anyone comes to me but loves his father, mother, wife, children, brothers, or sisters—or even life—more than me, he cannot be my follower" (Luke 14:26 NCV). Perpetua believed what Jesus said, and she wanted—more than anything else—to be His follower.

Perpetua was in prison for refusing to offer incense to honor the Roman gods. As a Christian, she would honor no other god than Jesus. The penalty for Perpetua's "crime" was death. She lived at a time when the Roman emperor wanted to stop people from becoming Christians and following Christ. Asking them to honor a false god was one way to discover the true Christians and get rid of them.

Perpetua had a family who loved her. She was a young married woman with a baby boy, a mom, dad, and brothers. And her family had plenty of money. She had so much to live for. If she denied being a Christian and honored a false god, then she would be free. But Perpetua refused.

Her dad visited her in prison. "Think of your brothers, think of your mother and your aunt, think of your child. . . . Give up your pride!" her father begged. It wasn't about pride—it was about loving Jesus and following Him, even if it meant loving Him more than her family. Perpetua felt sad when she said no to her father, but she chose to follow Jesus and give up everything else.

When her trial began, the Roman governor asked, "Will you honor the Roman gods?"

Perpetua said, "No."

"Are you a Christian?"

"Yes," she answered.

There was nothing left to say. Perpetua was killed.

Jesus wants us to love Him more than anyone or anything else. Could you be like Perpetua and give up everything for Him?

. . . .

"Have no gods other than me."
Exodus 20:3

128

Peter's Mother-In-Law
(Matthew 8:14–15; Mark 1:29–31; Luke 4:38–39)

Get Up and Go!

Peter's mother-in-law's story is another of those little stories in the Bible: "Jesus came to Peter's house. He saw Peter's wife's mother in bed. She was very sick. He touched her hand and the sickness left her. She got up and cared for Jesus" (Matthew 8:14–15).

While reading your Bible, you might read the story quickly and without thinking. But if you stop to wonder about Peter's mother-in-law, you'll discover that she has a lesson to share.

Have you ever felt like not even trying when a problem got in your way? Maybe the problem seemed so big that you wished you could get into bed, hide under the covers, and stay there forever. Some things in life will get you down and try to keep you down.

Peter's mother-in-law's problem was illness. Peter was bringing Jesus and some friends to her house. She had plenty to do before they arrived, but then she got sick, so sick that she went to bed. When Jesus and the others got there, she felt too sick to even get out of bed and greet them.

The Bible doesn't say how Peter felt when he saw nothing ready and his mother-in-law in bed. But it does tell us that Peter asked Jesus to heal her. Jesus only cared that sickness had beaten her down. He showed loving-kindness toward her and healed her problem. Jesus made her strong again, so she could get up and get going.

The lesson in her story is that Jesus can heal whatever gets you down. When you feel like giving up, it's Jesus who gives you strength to get up and keep going. Ask for His help. You can count on Him to care about your troubles and to show loving-kindness toward you—always.

He gives strength to the weak. And He gives power to him who has little strength.
Isaiah 40:29

ELIZABETH PRENTISS

(1818–78)

Good Enough

Elizabeth Prentiss grew up a sickly little girl. She once said she had never known what it felt like to be well. Elizabeth suffered from pain in her side, fainting spells, and headaches that upset her stomach. Every day something made her unwell. Her illnesses caused Elizabeth to feel gloomy, but she wore a happy face anyway. She put all her strength into living, and those around her saw a cheery girl with a sense of humor.

God gave Elizabeth a special talent—writing. Her mom understood that Elizabeth needed a quiet space where she could think and write. So she set up a special room in their house where Elizabeth could work.

As she wrote, Elizabeth discovered that she loved writing for kids. Some of her first stories and poems were published when Elizabeth was sixteen. Because she was Christian and loved God, Elizabeth wrote stories that she hoped would lead children—and adults too—to "do good." She found inspiration for her stories, poems, and songs in even the most difficult times of her life.

Sometimes Elizabeth thought she wasn't good enough. Even when she became a well-known author and hymn writer, Elizabeth felt she could never live up to what God expected from her. She fought hard against those feelings. She remained humble, never seeking fame for her work. Elizabeth wanted more of God. She wanted Him to fill up those places of self-doubt and gloom, so she put all her strength and energy into pleasing Him.

Do you sometimes feel like you're not good enough? God doesn't want you to feel that way. He loves you just as you are. If gloomy thoughts come into your head, fight against them like Elizabeth did. Ask God to fill you up with more of Him.

SO NOW, THOSE WHO ARE IN CHRIST JESUS ARE NOT JUDGED GUILTY.
ROMANS 8:1 NCV

Priscilla
(acts 18:1-3, 18-28)

Forever Friends

Who is your best friend? Have you wondered if God brought you two together? God has a way of putting people in the same place at the same time so they will meet. It was that way when Paul met his new friend Priscilla and her husband, Aquila.

Paul had been in Athens, Greece, sharing the Good News with those who would listen. Athens became a dangerous place for Christians. The leaders sent Paul to court because he spoke publicly about Jesus. So Paul decided to move to a nearby city, Corinth. Around the same time, Priscilla and Aquila also moved there. They had been living in Rome, but they were kicked out because Rome's emperor disliked Jews and wanted them removed from his city.

Maybe you met your best friend because you shared a common interest. That's how Paul met his new friends. Priscilla and Aquila worked as tentmakers. Paul made tents too! Making and selling tents was one way he earned money for his ministry. Priscilla and Aquila also were Christians like Paul.

The friends stayed together in Corinth. They made tents and spent time talking about the Bible. Paul knew a lot about the scriptures, and he was a good Bible teacher. Before long the three became forever friends.

Paul didn't stay in one place very long. He moved around, teaching about Jesus. When he decided to leave Corinth, Priscilla and Aquila went with him. They traveled together about 350 miles to Ephesus. After a while, the friends said goodbye. Priscilla and Aquila stayed there and shared the Good News, and Paul traveled on to reach more people for Jesus. They remained forever friends though, keeping in touch through letters.

Do you have a forever friend? Why do you think God put you together?

Some friends May ruin you, but a real friend will be More loyal than a brother.
PROVERBS 18:24 NCV

THE PROVERBS 31 WOMAN
(PROVERBS 31:10-31)

❧⁖ॐﻬ≼≼≼ⅇ

Wives and Moms

If you read Proverbs 31 in the Bible, you'll discover a mom giving advice to her grown son, a young king named Lemuel. His mom wants him to respect women, so she tells him the many things a good wife and mom does—the stuff kids and husbands might not notice. The king's mom had plenty of practice being a wife and raising children, so her advice is likely rooted in her own experience.

She tells Lemuel that a good wife and mom is worth more than rubies—she's priceless! She's trustworthy too, and everything she does is for her husband and kids. She manages the house and doesn't waste time. She makes sure her family has clean clothes to wear and good meals to eat.

In her own Bible-time words, the king's mom describes what today is grocery shopping and preparing breakfast and lunches to take to school: "She is like a trader's ship, bringing food from far away. She gets up while it is still dark and prepares food for her family" (Proverbs 31:14–15 NCV).

A Proverbs 31 woman knows how to manage finances. If she chooses to work, she does and brings money into the household. She stays up late at night caring for her family, and still she finds time to take care of herself. Most important, she loves and respects God, and others see Him through her. She is wise and helps her neighbors, the poor, and the needy.

At the end of her long list of what wives and moms do, the king's mom tells him to show respect for women, to praise his wife often, and to tell others how wonderful she is.

Do you know a Proverbs 31 woman? Think about all the wonderful things she does. Then tell her, "Thank you!"

· ·

SHE IS STRONG AND IS RESPECTED BY THE PEOPLE. SHE LOOKS FORWARD TO THE FUTURE WITH JOY.
PROVERBS 31:25 NCV

Jackie Pullinger
(1944–)

A Strong-Minded Woman

Jackie Pullinger is a woman with determination. If something needs fixing, she finds a way to get it done. Jackie works in Hong Kong helping drug addicts, gang members, and others find Jesus and turn their lives around.

Jackie always wanted to be a missionary. She went through the process of finding a church group or other organization to sponsor her, but her efforts failed. She had almost given up her dream of mission work in China when a minister at a church near where Jackie lived in London advised her to go anyway. The little money she had bought her a one-way ticket on the cheapest boat to Hong Kong.

Jackie took a job as a primary school teacher in the most dangerous part of the city, a rundown place of poorly built high-rise buildings. Drug dealers, addicts, and gang members lived there among families trying to live right. Crime was everywhere. Jackie saw right away that something had to be done to change things in this place called the Walled City.

She set up a youth center for teens, a safe place where they could have fun. She earned the trust of teens in the gangs, and she shared with them the Good News about Jesus. Some became Christians and turned their lives around for good.

Today Jackie has a special mission helping addicts get clean. With money that comes through volunteers and others who give generously, she started the St. Stephen's Society. Thanks to Jackie, there are safe places all around Hong Kong where people with addictions can get clean and learn about Jesus. The hope is that they grow to love Him and serve Him for the rest of their lives.

What have you learned from Jackie's story? What does it mean to have determination?

THE LORD GOD HELPS ME, SO I WILL NOT BE ASHAMED.
I WILL BE DETERMINED, AND I KNOW I WILL NOT BE DISGRACED.
ISAIAH 50:7 NCV

RaHaB
(JOSHUa 2; 6:17, 22–23)

Spies!

When the Israelites arrived at the land God promised them, they found the Canaanites living there. The Israelites politely asked them to leave, but most refused.

God wanted the Israelites there. The land belonged to them, and they had no choice but to fight for it.

The Israelites' leader, Joshua, sent two spies into the large city of Jericho. There was a woman living in Jericho who was well known in the city, and not in a good way. Rahab didn't live a godly life, but God needed her to help His people. She hid the spies in her house.

Someone saw the spies enter Rahab's house and told Jericho's king. It wasn't unusual for Rahab to entertain men, so the king thought maybe she didn't know they were spies. He sent a message telling her who the men were and ordering her to bring the men out. Rahab lied, "They've already gone."

When it was safe for the spies to leave, Rahab reminded them she had saved their lives. "So now, promise me before the LORD," she said, "that you will show kindness to my family just as I showed kindness to you" (Joshua 2:12 NCV). She asked the spies to promise that she and her family would be safe when the Israelites came and took the land.

The spies promised, and they stayed true to their word. When the Israelites destroyed everything in the city, they rescued Rahab and her family. They allowed the family to live safely in their land because Rahab had helped them.

God uses all kinds of people. Rahab didn't live a godly life, but she served God by helping the Israelites. In return God did what His spies promised. He saved the lives of Rahab and her family.

Think about it: When you make promises, do you keep them?

· ·

IT IS BETTER NOT TO MAKE a PROMISE, THAN TO MAKE a PROMISE aND NOT PaY IT.
ECCLESIASTES 5:5

ReBeKaH
(GENESIS 17:1–8; 25:19–27; 27:1–37)

What God Already Knew

Rebekah's story begins before her husband, Isaac, was born. God promised Isaac's dad, Abraham, that Abraham would have many descendants who would rule great nations. Some would become kings.

Isaac grew up and married Rebekah. They had twins, Jacob and Esau. Esau was the oldest.

God told Rebekah that her twins would grow up to lead different nations, one stronger than the other. The older twin would serve the younger. This was strange because leadership in a family normally passed from a father to his oldest son.

Rebekah wasn't a perfect mom. She loved the younger twin, Jacob, more than she loved Esau. When the twins were almost grown, Isaac, their dad, was old and nearly blind. Rebekah worried that when Isaac died, Esau would become head of their family. She didn't want that! She wanted Jacob to lead them. But for it to happen, Jacob needed his father's blessing—his father's words making him head of the family.

Rebekah planned to trick Isaac into giving his blessing to Jacob. She told Jacob to dress in Esau's clothes to appear more like his brother. Then Rebekah cooked Isaac's favorite dinner. Jacob took it to his dad. "Father, it's me, Esau," he lied. "I brought your favorite meal."

Isaac loved the son he thought was Esau and gave him his blessing. He said, "May nations serve you and peoples bow down to you. May you be master over your brothers" (Genesis 27:29 NCV).

Rebekah's story reminds us that God knows everything ahead of time. When God made His promise to Abraham, He already knew Rebekah would trick Isaac into giving his blessing to Jacob. God had already planned for Jacob's descendants to include King David, who ruled the great nation of Israel. And God knew who one of King David's descendants would be—Jesus!

....

LORD, YOU HAVE EXAMINED ME AND KNOW ALL ABOUT ME.
PSALM 139:1 NCV

RHODA
(ACTS 12:1-17)

Rhoda, Open the Door!

When your heart suddenly fills with joy, nothing else seems to matter. Rhoda was *that* happy. She heard Jesus' disciple Peter knocking at her door, and the sound of his voice filled her with joy.

Peter had been locked up in prison for talking about Jesus. King Herod, who hated Christians, planned to put Peter on trial and find him guilty. Until then Herod had sixteen soldiers with Peter. He lay on the floor in chains with a soldier on either side. More soldiers guarded the entrance to his prison cell. There was no way for Peter to escape—or was there?

An angel appeared to Peter. "Get up!" he said. When Peter got up, the chains fell off, but the soldiers didn't notice. "Put your coat on and follow me," said the angel. Peter obeyed. They walked past one soldier after another, and none of them saw! When they arrived at the gate that led out to the city, the gate opened by itself. Peter walked through. Then the angel disappeared. Was it a dream?

No, it wasn't. Peter went to the house where Rhoda lived. Christians were gathered there praying for Peter, thinking he was in prison and about to die. Peter knocked on the door. "It's me, Peter!" he called. Rhoda heard him, but she became so excited that she ran to tell the others without opening the door and letting Peter in. He kept knocking until finally someone noticed and opened the door.

Rhoda's story reminds us of something Jesus said: "See! I stand at the door and knock. If anyone hears My voice and opens the door, I will come in" (Revelation 3:20). We need not only to listen for Jesus' voice but also to open the doors to our hearts and let Him inside.

"BE LIKE SERVANTS WHO ARE WAITING FOR THEIR MASTER TO COME HOME FROM A WEDDING PARTY. WHEN HE COMES AND KNOCKS, THE SERVANTS IMMEDIATELY OPEN THE DOOR FOR HIM."
LUKE 12:36 NCV

HELEN ROSEVEARE
(1925–2016)

ᕷ᠁ᕪᘏ᠁ᘏᕷ

Whatever the Cost

When Helen Roseveare studied to become a doctor, she said, "I'll go anywhere God wants me to, whatever the cost." Think about that sentence. The first part about going anywhere might cause you to imagine all the wonderful places you could go. But what about the last part, "whatever the cost"? That's the scary part, the unknown. Helen didn't care. She trusted God. She planned to serve Him in the Congo (in Africa) as a missionary doctor for that country's people.

In the Congo, Helen worked hard, even making bricks to build small hospitals with thatched roofs where she could work to heal the sick. Her hands were torn and bleeding, but for Helen, it was worth it. Her suffering was nothing compared to what Jesus had suffered on the cross.

Within eleven years, the hospital grew and held a hundred beds. Thousands of patients were helped. Helen even started clinics to serve more people. By then she was tired. She took a break and went home to England.

After her rest, when Helen went back to Africa, she discovered things had changed. A civil war broke out. Many missionaries left, worried about their own safety. But Helen stayed. She was needed there. Nothing that could happen to her, she thought, could be worse than what Jesus had suffered.

Then trouble came. Enemy soldiers took over the hospital. They held Helen prisoner for five months. They robbed, beat, and shamed her through their actions and words. When it was over, Helen didn't know why these bad things happened to her, but still she knew that Jesus had suffered more. Instead of being angry, Helen thanked Jesus for allowing her to go through it, even though it almost cost her life.

Could you be like Helen, willing to serve God whatever the cost?

BUT IT IS NO SHAME TO SUFFER FOR BEING A CHRISTIAN.
PRAISE GOD FOR THE PRIVILEGE OF BEING CALLED BY HIS NAME!
1 PETER 4:16 NLT

RUTH
(RUTH 1:1–18)

Honor Your Mother and Father

We know that showing respect to moms and dads is important to God, because one of His Ten Commandments is "Honor your father and your mother" (Exodus 20:12).

When you read Ruth's story in the Bible, you will discover she was taught respect. She obeyed God's command. Ruth not only honored her own parents, but her husband's as well.

Ruth had grown up in a place called Moab. Her husband was from Bethlehem, a town about fifty miles away. He had moved to Moab with his parents when he was a boy. Life hadn't been easy for Ruth's husband. Before he came to Moab, his family had suffered through a famine—they had little food to eat. Then, after they moved, his father died.

Ruth and her husband were respectful to his mother, Naomi. They made sure she was taken care of. For a while, life was good. Then Ruth's husband died too!

Ruth and Naomi had only each other.

Naomi felt homesick for Bethlehem. She wanted to live there again, so Ruth and her mother-in-law packed their things and started walking. Ruth was willing to leave the place where she had lived all her life so Naomi wouldn't be alone.

On the way, Naomi understood how much Ruth was giving up to be with her. She said, "Go back home! God bless you for being so kind to me."

But Ruth refused to leave Naomi. She said, "Don't beg me to leave you or to stop following you. Where you go, I will go. Where you live, I will live. Your people will be my people, and your God will be my God. And where you die, I will die, and there I will be buried" (Ruth 1:16–17 NCV).

What an amazing example of honor and respect!

IF YOU RESPECT YOUR FATHER AND MOTHER, YOU WILL LIVE A LONG TIME
AND YOUR LIFE WILL BE FULL OF MANY GOOD THINGS.
EPHESIANS 6:3

Salome, James and John's Mother
(Matthew 20:20–28)

༺᠅᠅᠅᠅᠅᠅᠅᠅᠅᠅᠅᠅༻

Aunt Salome

Salome understood who Jesus was. She believed He was the Christ, and that when He went back to His Father in heaven He would be the King of kings. She knew Him well because she was His aunt, a sister to Jesus' mother, Mary.

Like all moms, Salome wanted the best for her kids. Jesus had chosen her sons, James and John, as two of His twelve closest followers—His disciples. They were His cousins, and Jesus was teaching them along with the others that He would die but three days later be raised back to life. He was training them to teach others about Him after He went back to heaven.

Salome must have been proud of her sons. She knew they were special, chosen by Jesus. But Salome wanted something more for them. She wanted James and John to have a special place in heaven when they got there.

She went to her nephew Jesus with a request. Although she was His aunt, Salome honored Him as Lord and knelt before Him. James and John were with her.

"Say that my two sons may sit, one at Your right side and one at Your left side, when You are King," Salome said (Matthew 20:21).

Jesus answered, "The places at My right side and at My left side are not Mine to give. Whoever My Father says will have those places" (verse 23).

Jesus went on to say that kings and other important people sometimes show off their power over others. "Don't be like that," He told His aunt, cousins, and the other disciples. "What's more important is showing that you care for others."

Salome's story reminds us that we might not always get from God what we ask for. He knows best what we need.

• •

Or if you do ask, you do not receive because your reasons for asking are wrong. You want these things only to please yourselves.

JAMES 4:3

SaMSON'S MOTHEr
(JUDGeS 13:1–24)

She Saw Something Amazing

The Bible doesn't tell us the names of all the people in its stories. Samson's mom is one of them. Still, we shouldn't skip over those people and think they aren't important. Each of them has something to teach us.

Samson's mom is mentioned in the Bible only as Manoah's wife. She and her husband had no children. But then an angel from the Lord showed himself to her. She wasn't sure whether he really was an angel. Maybe he was a prophet—a real person who spoke God's words.

The angel said that soon she would have a son. From the day the baby was born, he would belong to God. His mother was not to cut his hair. The angel said that her baby would grow up to help set the Israelites free from their enemies, the Philistines. He also told Samson's mom what things she shouldn't eat and drink while she was expecting.

When Samson's mom told her husband about the angel, he didn't totally believe her. So he prayed and asked God to send the "man" back. God answered his prayer. This time the angel showed himself to both Manoah and his wife.

When the angel left them, Manoah believed, and he felt afraid. "We have seen an angel!" he said. "Now, we are going to die!"

Samson's mom had a more positive view of what seeing the angel meant. She had faith that God wasn't going to kill them even though they saw His angel. Instead, she saw the deeper meaning that God trusted them enough to show them something amazing. God chose them to bring a son into the world who would help save Israel from its enemies.

How do you think you would feel if God trusted you enough to show you an angel?

. . . .

"WHOeVer Can Be TrusTeD WITH a LITTLe Can aLso Be TrusTeD WITH a LoT,
aND WHOeVer Is DIsHONesT WITH a LITTLe Is DIsHONesT WITH a LoT."
LUKe 16:10 NCV

Sarah
(GENESIS 17:15-17, 19; 18:10-15; 21:1-7)

She Laughed

Imagine God promising you something that seemed impossible. Would you trust Him to keep His promise, or might you laugh and say, "There's no way that can happen"?

Abraham laughed at God's promise when God said He would bless Abraham and his wife, Sarah, with a son. What was so funny? Abraham was one hundred years old. Sarah was ninety. For as long as they were married, Abraham and Sarah had wanted kids. Now here they were in their old age and finally—well, who had ever heard of such a thing? Not only did God promise them a son, but He also said their son would have children and grandchildren who would grow up to lead great nations. Yes, Abraham laughed.

Sarah overheard the promise, and she laughed too.

When God heard Sarah laugh, He asked Abraham, "Why did Sarah laugh? Is anything too hard for me?"

Sarah felt afraid because she had laughed at God, so she lied: "I didn't laugh."

"Yes, you did laugh," God said.

Although they had laughed at God's promise and showed that their faith in Him wasn't perfect, God did what He promised. About a year later, Sarah gave birth to a healthy baby boy. When she held her baby boy, Sarah laughed once more, but this time not because God's promise seemed impossible. Sarah laughed with joy that God, with all His power, is able to do the impossible!

Sarah's story is one of many in the Bible where God does what seems out of the question. But if you believe in God's power to do anything, you will always have hope. You'll look around and see all the amazing things He does and laugh with joy because your God, the one and only God, can work miracles. He does what no one else can do.

- -

"FOR GOD CAN DO ALL THINGS."
LUKE 1:37

EDITH SCHAEFFER
(1914–2013)

Everyone Is Welcome

How I know Jesus is not the Son of God, and how I know that the Bible is not the Word of God"—this was the subject of a speech delivered at a youth group meeting Edith attended. She believed Jesus is God's Son. She trusted the Bible as His Word. So Edith stood and disagreed with the speaker. At the same time, a boy across the room stood up and disagreed too.

That was how Edith met her husband, Francis Schaeffer. Neither knew then what God had planned for them. God would bless them with four children and send their family to Switzerland where Edith and Francis would work as missionaries.

They settled into a home in a quiet valley in the mountains. The couple worked setting up ministries for children. Their daughter suggested they have classes in their home so people in their little village could learn about Jesus. But the village leaders didn't like the Schaeffers sharing their religious views, so they made them leave.

The family moved to another village in the Swiss mountains, and there they opened their home to anyone who wanted to come talk about God and have their questions answered. Francis and Edith asked God to send those who needed to know Him. People began hearing about the Schaeffers, and they came to stay as guests at L'Abri—the name of their home.

Edith and Francis never judged those who came. All were welcome. Edith showed them love and hospitality. She cooked, cleaned, and shared with guests the truth that God is real and ever present in their everyday lives. The ministry at L'Abri grew and continues today.

Edith's story is a great example of Christian hospitality—welcoming, warm, and nonjudgmental—the way Jesus is!

What do you think it means to show hospitality to others?

DO NOT FORGET TO BE KIND TO STRANGERS AND LET THEM STAY IN YOUR HOME.
SOME PEOPLE HAVE HAD ANGELS IN THEIR HOMES WITHOUT KNOWING IT.
HEBREWS 13:2

Ida Scudder

(1870–1960)

Doctor Ida

Ida Scudder's family included many missionary doctors in India. Ida's dad was one of them. While living in India with her family, Ida saw how poor, sick, and hungry the people were. She wanted to get away, to go back home to America. No way did Ida want to be a medical missionary and carry on her family's work.

When her dad became ill, Ida felt happy to return to America with her family. When he was well enough to return to India, Ida stayed in the states and attended college. She hoped to get married, but then plans changed.

Her mom wasn't feeling well. Ida's dad needed Ida to come to India and help with their work. So she went. While there she saw three women die because they wanted to be treated by a female doctor and there was none. At that moment, Ida's life changed. Now she wanted to become a doctor and help people in India. Ida knew it was God's plan.

She went back to America and got her medical degree. Then Dr. Ida returned to India. Traveling in a cart pulled by oxen, she brought medical supplies and care to small villages. She set up clinics and a hospital, and she trained women to become nurses. But that wasn't enough for Ida. She wanted to do more for the Indian people, so she started a medical school where women, and later men, learned to be doctors. The school exists today. The Christian Medical College and Hospital is one of the top-ranked medical schools in India.

Jesus said, "If anyone wants to follow Me, he must give up himself and his own desires. He must take up his cross everyday and follow Me" (Luke 9:23). What do you think that means? Did Ida follow His command?

· ·

"IF YOU REFUSE TO TAKE UP YOUR CROSS AND FOLLOW ME, YOU ARE NOT WORTHY OF BEING MINE. IF YOU CLING TO YOUR LIFE, YOU WILL LOSE IT; BUT IF YOU GIVE UP YOUR LIFE FOR ME, YOU WILL FIND IT."
MATTHEW 10:38–39 NLT

SHIPHRaH aND PUaH
(EXODUS 1:8-21)

The Nurses Who Saved Israel

Shiphrah and Puah lived when God's people, the Israelites, were slaves under the rule of Egypt's pharaoh. He was considered the greatest ruler in the world back then—and he wasn't a nice guy. Pharaoh decided the Israelites were becoming too many. He worried that as their families grew there might be enough men to overthrow his government and escape from Egypt. So Pharaoh made a terrible rule. He commanded that all baby boys born to the Israelites be killed!

Shiphrah and Puah were midwives—nurses who helped women when they had babies. One day Pharaoh called them to come to him. He said, "When an Israelite woman gives birth, if the baby is a girl, let her live. If it's a boy, kill him!"

The women had to decide: would they obey Pharaoh, or would they disobey and allow the boys to live? The Bible doesn't say whether Shiphrah and Puah were Egyptians or Israelites, but it does say they feared God. Pharaoh had power over them to decide whether they lived or died if they disobeyed. But God had power over them too—more power, they decided, than Pharaoh. So Shiphrah and Puah secretly allowed the baby boys to live and their mothers to hide them.

When Pharaoh found out Israelite baby boys were alive, he sent for the nurses. "Why have you disobeyed me?" he asked.

"Because the women give birth before we can get there," they lied.

God blessed Shiphrah and Puah for obeying Him. He gave them families of their own. And because of these two nurses, the Israelites grew in number. One baby they saved was Moses, and when he grew up, he led the Israelites out of Egypt.

Do you believe that Shiphrah and Puah were right to obey God instead of Pharaoh?

....

IT IS a HaTED THING FOr KINGS TO DO WHaT IS WrONG, FOr a THrONE IS BUILT ON WHaT IS rIGHT.
PROVERBS 16:12

THE SHUNAMMITE WOMAN
(2 KINGS 4:8-37)

A Blessing

God often blesses us through the actions of others. The Shunammite woman's story is about how God blessed her through His prophet Elisha. We don't know the woman's name—the Bible doesn't tell us. But we do know that she was an important woman living in a small village called Shunem.

The woman understood that Elisha was a holy man of God. Whenever he came to the village, she made food for him to eat. She and her husband created a little room for Elisha on the second floor of their house, so that when Elisha came to Shunem he would have a nice place to stay.

Elisha wanted to reward the woman for her hospitality, so he asked what he could do for her. The woman said she had everything she needed—but Elisha's servant told Elisha that the woman and her husband had no son. It seemed impossible Elisha could change this. But Elisha knew God could do anything. "At this time next year you will hold a son in your arms," Elisha said (2 Kings 4:16).

God did exactly what Elisha predicted. He gave the woman and her husband a son.

Years later the boy suffered a terrible headache, and he died. His mother carried him up to Elisha's room and laid him on Elisha's bed. Then she got on a donkey and rushed to find Elisha. She begged the prophet to return home with her.

The woman and Elisha hurried to where the boy's body lay. Elisha shut the door and prayed. Then Elisha lay down, spreading his body over the boy's. That's when God did a miracle through Elisha. He made the boy alive again!

The Shunammite woman felt so grateful. She fell down at Elisha's feet and thanked him.

Has God ever blessed you through the actions of someone else?

. . . .

"YOU WILL BE A BLESSING TO OTHERS."
GENESIS 12:2 NCV

Mary Slessor
(1848–1915)

Merciful Mary

Mary Slessor was a Scottish missionary in Africa. She dared to go deep into the areas where native African tribes lived. Few missionaries had the courage to go there, especially women. They feared they wouldn't survive.

Superstition existed everywhere among the tribes, and they were preoccupied with demons, spirits, and false gods. One of their worst beliefs was that if a woman gave birth to twins, the second-born was possessed—controlled by an evil spirit. If a mom had twins, the tribes abandoned her and the babies and left them in the jungle to die.

Mary believed only in the one true God, and her mission was to show mercy to those who were treated badly because of false beliefs. Mary opened up a house for the twins who were left behind. Some of the moms came too. Mary cared for them and treated the children as if they were her own.

She knew that if she were to help the tribes, she needed to live among them. Mary risked her life to learn their language and blend in with them. She wasn't afraid to let them know when she disagreed with their ways, but at the same time she became their friend. She participated in their good customs, laughed with them, and ate their food. The tribes learned not only to accept her, but also to respect and love her. Mary taught them about Jesus, and even when they were not accepting of Him, she was merciful—kind and caring—toward them.

If you think about it, you'll discover that you have something in common with those tribes. You likely don't practice superstitions, but you do other things that displease God. Still, like Mary, God is merciful toward you, forgiving you for your faults and loving you anyway.

FOR YOU ARE GOOD AND READY TO FORGIVE, O LORD.
YOU ARE RICH IN LOVING-KINDNESS TO ALL WHO CALL TO YOU.
PSALM 86:5

SUSANNAH SPURGEON
(1832–1903)

Worth More Than Rubies

The Bible says, "Who can find a good wife? For she is worth far more than rubies" (Proverbs 31:10). Susannah Spurgeon was that kind of wife.

Married to a famous pastor in London, Susannah quickly learned that she would never be as important to her husband as God was to him. Charles Spurgeon always had something to do for his church, and at times Susannah felt left out. But after talking with her mother, Susannah decided it was right for her to become Charles's helper instead of complaining that he didn't spend enough time with her. She joined him in making God *their* priority.

After giving birth to twin boys, Susannah became weak. She often was sick in bed and not very strong. Still, she did what she could to serve God, her husband, and their sons.

While Charles went about his work, Susannah raised their sons. She taught them the Bible and what it means to be Christian. She shared in their joy when both boys accepted Jesus as their Savior.

Charles wrote sermons and books about being a Christian, and Susannah proofread his work. One day while editing a book, Susannah wished she could give a copy to every minister in England. (In the 1800s, when Susannah lived, many pastors were poor and had no money to buy books.) Charles encouraged her to find a way to do it.

She started a charity called the Book Fund. With her own money, Susannah mailed a hundred books to pastors in need. The Book Fund became her purpose and life's work. By the time Susannah died, her charity had provided almost two hundred thousand books to Christians throughout England.

Do you think Susannah was content being her husband's helper? Do you think it was right for Charles to put God first?

· ·

Her husband trusts her completely. With her, he has everything he needs.
PROVERBS 31:11 NCV

Patricia St. John
(1919–93)

Children's Book Author

Patricia St. John's family lived in the beautiful English countryside and later in Switzerland. Although Patricia was young when she lived there, memories of these places stayed with her the rest of her life.

The daughter of missionaries, Patricia grew up knowing Jesus. When just six years old, she remembered a Bible verse, Isaiah 43:1, in which God says, "I have called you by name. You are Mine!" Patricia responded by praying: "God, if you want me, I'm Yours." Of course God wanted her! He already had her life planned.

World War II had begun when Patricia finished high school. She decided to help her country by becoming a nurse. During the war, Patricia worked as a nurse in London.

When the war ended, her life took a different turn. She helped her aunt run a girls' boarding school. Before the girls went to sleep each night, Patricia enjoyed telling them bedtime stories. Her stories were so good that she wrote them down. She soon understood that God had given her the gift of writing. She realized she could write children's stories that were exciting and fun to read and that also taught kids about God.

But God had something more planned. Patricia's brother ran a mission hospital in Morocco. Many women there did not want to be treated by male doctors, so Patricia went to help her brother provide medical care. She learned the people's language and told them Bible stories. Because of her storytelling, many came to know Jesus as their Savior.

When Patricia returned to England, she wrote children's books based on her life experiences. You might enjoy reading them. Look for *Star of Light*, *The Tanglewoods' Secret*, *The Secret at Pheasant Cottage*, *Rainbow Garden*, *Treasures of the Snow*, and *Where the River Begins*.

THERE IS A SPECIAL TIME FOR EVERYTHING. THERE IS A TIME FOR EVERYTHING THAT HAPPENS UNDER HEAVEN.
ECCLESIASTES 3:1

BETTY STAM
(1906–34)

Something Worthwhile

Betty Scott was an American whose parents were missionaries in China. While attending school in America, Betty planned to return to China and become a missionary. One day she wrote, "I want something really worthwhile to live for. . . . I want it to be God's choice for me and not my own."

Betty met her future husband, John Stam, while they were students at Moody Bible Institute in Chicago. The couple married after they returned to China to do mission work.

It was a time when Communists plotted to overthrow the Chinese government. The Communists hated Christians, and missionaries were in danger. By then, Betty and John had been in China for a while, and they had a six-month-old daughter. When word came that Communist soldiers were nearby, the Stams didn't have time to get out before the soldiers arrived at their door.

Betty and John welcomed them into their home with the same kindness Jesus might have. The soldiers took advantage of their hospitality and then kidnapped Betty, John, and their baby. The Communists put them in prison and demanded a ransom—money—for their release. But Betty and her husband knew their mission headquarters wouldn't pay a ransom. That would only encourage more kidnappings. Still, they had peace in their hearts that even if they died for being Christians, their service to God would have been worthwhile.

The ending of Betty's story is not a happy one. Their baby's life was spared, but the Communists murdered Betty and John. Their story spread around the world and touched the hearts of many. It led some to become missionaries themselves to carry on the work Betty and John had begun.

Betty lost her life bringing God's Word to the Chinese people. Do you think her life was worthwhile?

"DO NOT BE AFRAID OF WHAT YOU WILL SUFFER. LISTEN! THE DEVIL WILL THROW SOME OF YOU INTO PRISON TO TEST YOU. . . . BE FAITHFUL EVEN TO DEATH. THEN I WILL GIVE YOU THE CROWN OF LIFE."

REVELATION 2:10

ANNE STEELE
(1717-78)

A Song in Her Heart

Songwriters are poets and storytellers. They are somewhat like authors because they put their words on paper, but they set their words to music. Often they write songs about their own feelings or about things that really happened to them.

Anne Steele was a British songwriter and poet in the 1700s. Life wasn't easy for her, but she always did her best to have a cheerful attitude. Her mom died when Anne was just three years old. When Anne was a teenager, she got malaria and suffered from it for the rest of her life. Still, Anne chose to look on the bright side. She often entertained her friends by reading them poems she had written. Her poems were good—good enough to be set to music and shared with the world. But "Nanny," as her friends and family called her, was not eager to publish them. She was humble, not wanting attention drawn to herself. Anne would be in her forties before she agreed to share her work with others.

She lived a quiet life, often preferring to be alone. She never married. Anne was engaged to and almost married the love of her life, but he drowned before their wedding happened. Anne received other marriage proposals, but she decided that a single life was what she wanted.

Anne finally published her poetry and essays using a pen name, Theodosia, and she gave the money she earned to charities. The hymns she wrote became very popular, especially in Baptist churches. She wrote 144 hymns, many poems and essays, and became known as "the mother of the English hymn." Some of Anne's hymns are included in hymnals still used in churches today.

Do you have a song in your heart? Don't be afraid to share it. Sing it to the Lord!

SING TO THE LORD A NEW SONG. LET ALL THE EARTH SING TO THE LORD. SING TO THE LORD. HONOR HIS NAME. MAKE HIS SAVING POWER KNOWN FROM DAY TO DAY.
PSALM 96:1-2

JONI EaReCKSON TaDa
(1949–)

Walking with Jesus

If you met Joni, she might tell you there are things more important than being able to walk or use your hands. Joni knows! She's been in a wheelchair for fifty years, unable to walk and with hands that barely work. She was perfectly well until a diving accident changed her life, paralyzing her at age seventeen. Joni might also tell you, "I really would rather be in this wheelchair knowing Jesus as I do than be on my feet without Him."

Knowing Jesus—putting faith and trust in Him—is the one thing that got Joni through the worst experience of her life. Now she serves God by helping others with disabilities. Her positive attitude is contagious. With Jesus' help, she works hard trying to give hope to those facing physical challenges.

In 1979 Joni started a worldwide ministry called Joni and Friends to aid those affected by disabilities. She hosts radio and television programs in which she shares God's Word and positive stories of others living with disabilities. Joni has written more than forty books, recorded albums of songs, and even starred in a movie about her life.

Being disabled hasn't stopped her from living a full, rich life. Joni married the love of her life, Ken Tada. She travels the world, gives speeches, serves on committees, and reaches out to young people with recent life-changing disabilities.

Life wasn't always easy for Joni. She knows what it feels like to be depressed, to wish the accident never happened, and even to doubt God. But she would tell you that God has never let her down. Instead, He uses her to lead others with disabilities out of their depression and into a joyful Christian life.

Do you know someone with a disability? How can you help?

....

[THE LORD] ANSWERED ME, "I AM ALL YOU NEED. . . . MY POWER WORKS BEST IN WEAK PEOPLE."
I AM HAPPY TO BE WEAK AND HAVE TROUBLES SO I CAN HAVE CHRIST'S POWER IN ME.
2 CORINTHIANS 12:9

Maria Taylor
(1837–70)

Missionary to China

Maria's parents, British missionaries, served the Chinese people in several countries. Maria was born while they were in Malaysia. For the first nine years of her life, Maria and her family lived among the Chinese and learned their culture. So, to Maria this felt like home.

Sadly, by the time she was nine, both of Maria's parents had died. She, along with her sister and brother, went to live with an uncle in England.

All the time she was in England, Maria wanted to return "home" to China. So, when she turned sixteen, Maria and her sister went back and worked at a girls' school run by a friend of their mother. It was there Maria fell in love with and married a British missionary, Hudson Taylor.

Maria and Hudson got busy ministering to the Chinese people. Maria started an elementary school. She spoke the children's language, so teaching was easy. The couple took in and cared for several Chinese children. They even operated a hospital.

But then Hudson became ill. The Taylors were forced to return to England so he could recover. This was part of God's plan! While in England, Hudson asked God for twenty-four missionaries to go back to China with him and Maria. God answered his prayer. The mission team boarded a clipper ship and headed out to sea. The trip wasn't easy. Two typhoons—terrible storms—almost sunk the ship. But prayer and faith in God kept the missionaries safe.

Back "home" in China, Maria worked with the female missionaries who had come with them. She trained them to understand the Chinese and to serve them and teach them about Jesus. Together they led many to give their lives to Christ.

What have you learned about missionaries? Would you like to be one someday?

• •

HOW BEAUTIFUL ON THE MOUNTAINS ARE THE FEET OF THE MESSENGER WHO BRINGS GOOD NEWS,
THE GOOD NEWS OF PEACE AND SALVATION, THE NEWS THAT THE GOD OF ISRAEL REIGNS!
ISAIAH 52:7 NLT

CORRIE TEN BOOM
(1892–1983)

Corrie's Closet

Corrie grew up in the Netherlands, near Amsterdam. Her Christian family welcomed friends, neighbors, and even strangers into their home. Corrie's dad held prayer meetings at their house. He often prayed for the Jewish people, whom he believed were God's chosen people, as told in the Old Testament.

During World War II, Nazi soldiers arrested Jews for no other reason than they were Jewish. The Nazis put them in prison camps—called "concentration camps"—where they suffered terribly and died.

The ten Boom family wanted to help the Jews. So Corrie and her family became part of something called the "Dutch underground." Corrie and her sister Betsie helped Jews escape from the Nazis by hiding them in their home. If the Nazis ever came to the house, the ten Booms planned for their Jewish "guests" to hide in a secret place behind a closet, just big enough for six.

One day someone told the Nazis what the ten Booms were doing. The Nazis arrested the entire ten Boom family, but the Jews hiding in the closet were not found and later escaped.

Corrie and Betsie were put in a concentration camp where they were treated poorly. Still, they held secret worship services using a Bible they had managed to sneak in. Betsie died in the camp, but Corrie survived. She returned to her home in the Netherlands and continued to help people in need. She even forgave the soldiers who had been cruel to her in the camp.

Corrie traveled the world speaking about her experience with the Nazis. She wrote about it in a bestselling book called *The Hiding Place.* Today almost everyone knows her name. Her story is one of the most famous to come from World War II.

Can you think of one word that best describes Corrie?

I WILL SAY TO THE LORD, "YOU ARE MY SAFE AND STRONG PLACE, MY GOD, IN WHOM I TRUST."
PSALM 91:2

Saint Teresa of Avila
(1515–82)

A Woman of Faith

What does it mean to have lukewarm faith? If something is lukewarm, it is neither hot nor cold. It might even be described as average. If someone's faith in God is average, that's not such a good thing! God is way above average. He's perfect—and He deserves the most powerful, on-fire faith humans can give.

Teresa of Avila lived the first forty years of her life having lukewarm faith. At age twenty-one, she entered a convent that was quite open-minded. The nuns were allowed to have their own belongings, and they could mingle with people outside the convent. Not focusing entirely on God, Teresa believed, had caused her faith to weaken.

One day while walking in the convent, Teresa noticed a statue of Jesus on the cross. She saw it in a way she hadn't before, and she felt Christ's powerful love for her. From that day forward, Teresa's faith grew. It became so strong that she gave up everything else that mattered. She put worldly things in the past and gave all her attention to the Lord.

Quiet prayer was important to Teresa. She wanted to start convents for women and monasteries for men where they could dedicate their lives to prayer and serving God. Teresa had a God-given gift to lead, and she made those convents and monasteries happen.

Teresa also had the gift of understanding the spiritual life. She wrote down her ideas about prayer and living for God. Even today, more than four hundred years later, her spiritual writings are read and studied.

Rest didn't come easy for Teresa. She dedicated every day of her life to serving the Lord, and she is an outstanding example of strong, on-fire faith.

How would you rate your faith—is it on fire or is it lukewarm?

LEAD THEM IN THE RIGHT WAY SO THEY WILL HAVE STRONG FAITH.
Titus 1:13

SAINT TERESA OF CALCUTTA
(MOTHER TERESA)
(1910–97)

Servant to the Poor

Saint Teresa of Calcutta began her life as a little girl named Agnes. Born in Macedonia to a Catholic family, Agnes longed to become a nun and work helping the poor, especially the poor people in India.

At age eighteen, she left home and traveled to Ireland where a group of nuns, the Sisters of Loretto, trained her for work as a nun in India. A new name was given to her, Sister Mary Teresa.

Her first work in India was teaching at a convent school in Calcutta. While there, she took her final vows to become a nun, and she received the name most people know her by today—Mother Teresa.

Her desire to work with the poor grew even stronger. She felt Jesus telling her to leave the school and work directly with the poorest of the poor. She followed His words and went into the Calcutta slums. There she nursed the sick, fed the hungry, and brought love to those who felt lonely and forgotten. Some teachers and students she met while teaching at the convent school joined in, helping Mother Teresa with her work. As more came to volunteer, the group became known as the Missionaries of Charity.

News of Mother Teresa's work spread around the world. She received many awards, including the Nobel Peace Prize. But her most amazing honor came after her death when the Catholic Church made her a saint.

Throughout her life, Mother Teresa struggled with her relationship with God. She wanted so much more of Him in her heart. She felt distant from Him. In that way, she was like King David in the Bible, who cried out to God, "How long will You hide from me?" (Read Psalm 13.)

Can you think of some ways to help the poor in your community?

HAPPY IS THE MAN WHO CARES FOR THE POOR. THE LORD WILL SAVE HIM IN TIMES OF TROUBLE.
PSALM 41:1

Lilias Trotter
(1853–1928)

She Had to Choose

From the beginning, when God created Adam, He gave humans the gift of freedom. We are allowed so many choices, even whether to love God or not. Sometimes the most difficult choice is when we have to choose between two things so wonderful, awesome, and amazing—so attractive that words can't describe them. That was the kind of choice Lilias had to make.

Lilias was born with the gift of creating art. Her talent was so great that she might have become one of England's best artists of the nineteenth century. But Lilias also had a heart dedicated to God. She felt Him calling her to serve as a missionary in North Africa. She needed to choose between putting all her effort into her art, and likely becoming famous, or serving the Lord.

Lilias chose to serve God.

The North African Mission group turned down her request to serve with them. So Lilias went to Africa on her own, traveling with two friends. She didn't know anyone in North Africa, nor did she know the language spoken there.

Over the next forty years, Lilias traveled, often by camel, along the North African coast and into the Sahara Desert. She set up mission stations—places where missionaries lived and worked. Wherever she went, Lilias carried the Word of God to the people, and many came to know Him.

She didn't give up art completely. Lilias kept journals of her travels, and she filled the pages with her beautiful work. She had given up fame to serve God, but Lilias felt content. Once she painted cottony, white seeds drifting away from a dried dandelion head. For Lilias this represented emptying herself, giving herself fully to God.

Have you had to choose between two wonderful things? Which did you choose and why?

CHOOSE MY INSTRUCTION RATHER THAN SILVER, AND KNOWLEDGE RATHER THAN PURE GOLD.
Proverbs 8:10 NLT

SOJOURNER TRUTH
(1797–1883)

A Leader for Civil Rights

Sojourner Truth was born a slave. Her given name was Isabella. When she was nine, her owner sold her along with a flock of sheep for one hundred dollars. Can you imagine being separated from your family and sold? That sort of life was common for African-Americans when Isabella was young.

When she was about thirty years old, the state of New York began allowing slaves the freedom to leave and live on their own. Isabella's owner didn't want to free her, so she escaped. She didn't know then that God would use her to fight for equal rights for everyone, especially women and African-Americans.

As a free woman, she worked as a housekeeper and also did missionary work among the poor in New York City. Strong in her Christian faith, Isabella became a traveling preacher. She believed that God wanted her to take the name Sojourner Truth. (A sojourner is someone who travels from place to place.) She traveled about, preaching the truth from God's Word.

Sojourner knew what it meant to fight for freedom. She recognized that African-Americans and all women didn't enjoy the same freedoms as, for example, white men. It wasn't proper for women in her time to speak publicly about their views, but Sojourner didn't care. She stood up and spoke her mind. She fought through her words and actions to free the slaves in America and also for equal rights for women. At the end of the Civil War, when slavery became illegal in America, Sojourner helped newly freed slaves adapt to living free.

She is remembered today as a powerful leader for civil rights and as an example of someone who trusted God and wasn't afraid.

Is there a cause you feel strongly about? What can you do to make a difference?

"YOU WILL KNOW THE TRUTH AND THE TRUTH WILL MAKE YOU FREE."
JOHN 8:32

HARRIET TUBMAN
(1820–1913)

The Moses of Her People

If you know the story of Moses in the Bible, then it's easy to understand why Harriet Tubman was called the Moses of her people. The Bible tells us how Moses led God's people, the Israelites, out of slavery in Egypt. Many years later, Harriet led *her* people, African-Americans, out of slavery too.

In Harriet's time, Americans in the North and South were divided about the idea of slavery. Kindhearted people helped slaves escape through something called the Underground Railroad. This wasn't a real railroad, but a series of safe places where those who cared hid slaves as they escaped from states where slavery was legal.

After years of abuse by her master, Harriet managed to escape. She traveled at night, following the North Star. After a long journey and sheltering at railroad houses along the way, Harriet reached freedom. But it was not enough for her to be free. Now she knew the way out! Harriet went back—again and again—to help her family members and other slaves escape and follow her home. She used coded songs to communicate with the slaves and also with people in the Underground Railroad. To others, the words sounded like praise songs to the Lord. But to those participating in the escape, the lyrics provided special instructions.

Harriet remained persistent and courageous, risking her life to free others. She trusted God for her safety while helping about three hundred slaves escape to freedom. Today she is remembered as the most famous leader of the Underground Railroad. Her story is taught in schools, and in 2020 her portrait will replace President Andrew Jackson's on the front of America's twenty-dollar bills.

Read Exodus 14 in your Bible. Then answer this question: In what ways was Harriet Tubman like Moses?

YOU WERE CHOSEN TO BE FREE. BE CAREFUL THAT YOU DO NOT PLEASE YOUR OLD SELVES BY SINNING BECAUSE YOU ARE FREE. LIVE THIS FREE LIFE BY LOVING AND HELPING OTHERS.
GALATIANS 5:13

Mary Verghese
(1925–86)

God's Grace

Have you heard the words "God's grace" and wondered what they mean? His grace is when God shows His unconditional love for us, His kindness in circumstances even when we don't deserve it. We don't have to do anything to earn God's grace. He gives it to us for no other reason than He loves us.

Mary Verghese is someone who received God's grace and then used it to help others. She had just become a medical doctor in her home country, India, when a car accident left Mary's legs paralyzed. At first she felt sorry for herself. "God, why couldn't You have let me die?" she prayed. But God didn't want her to die. He had great plans for Mary's life. His grace would see her through the worst days and lead her into a promising future. Mary fought hard to overcome her disability. Still, she was confined to a wheelchair.

People in India suffered from leprosy, and a doctor friend suggested that Mary might be helpful to them. They would see that she had suffered a serious injury and that she still had hope for her future. Her hope could encourage others.

God's grace—His kindness—flowed through Mary to her patients. She brightened their days and made them smile. With God's grace, Mary learned to perform surgeries while sitting in her wheelchair. She dedicated her career as a doctor to helping her patients live as best they could with their disabilities. Mary even started the first center in India to treat people with leprosy and injuries to the spine and brain.

Mary trusted in God's love and grace and His promise that all things work together for good for those who love Him (Romans 8:28).

Has God used His grace to bring you through a difficult time?

"MY LIFE IS WORTH NOTHING TO ME UNLESS I USE IT FOR FINISHING THE WORK ASSIGNED ME BY THE LORD JESUS—THE WORK OF TELLING OTHERS THE GOOD NEWS ABOUT THE WONDERFUL GRACE OF GOD."
ACTS 20:24 NLT

JUDITH WEINBERG
(C. 1898–?)

❧⟡⟡⟡⟡⟡❧

She Changed Her Mind

Have you changed your mind about something after you decided wrong? Judith Weinberg changed her mind. As a result, she lost everything dear to her in this world—but she found something better.

Judith grew up a Russian Jew. As a child, she questioned her faith after she overheard her grandpa discussing whether Jesus was really God's Son or a fake. (Many Jews believe that Jesus was not God's promised Messiah.) As Judith heard the story of Jesus, she felt sorry that He was killed for doing nothing wrong. She couldn't get it out of her mind. She kept thinking and wondering about Him.

In 1914 war came to Russia. The Weinbergs lived close to the heaviest fighting near the German border, so they left their home, bringing with them very little. They started a new life farther into Russia.

After a while, Judith met and planned to marry a Jewish boy named Solomon. Judith still wondered about Jesus, so she convinced Solomon to go with her to services at a Christian church. There Judith's heart filled with love for Christ, and she accepted Him as her Savior. It cost Judith her fiancé and her family—they hated that she became a Christian, and they disowned her.

People in Russia were dying and suffering because of the war. So Judith and other Christians went into the villages to help and preach about Jesus. One day soldiers came into a prayer meeting Judith led. When they heard her say they were sinners and needed Jesus, the soldiers hated her words. They killed Judith for being a Christian. Still, she died not regretting her decision. Judith knew Jesus was real and that she was going to live with Him forever in heaven.

Do you think Judith made the right choice to become a Christian?

· ·

"YOU ARE THE CHRIST, THE SON OF THE LIVING GOD."
MATTHEW 16:16

SUSANNA WESLEY
(1669–1742)

An Excellent Mom

Can you imagine having twenty-four older siblings? That was how Susanna Wesley's life in England began. She was the youngest of twenty-five kids! And when she grew up, Susanna had nineteen kids of her own.

As a grown-up, Susanna knew the meaning of hardship. Nine of her children died when they were babies. Susanna's husband, Samuel, a pastor, was not the best provider. He had left the family for more than a year, and he wasn't good with money. His money problems twice sent him to jail. If that wasn't bad enough, their house burned down twice, and after the second fire the kids lived in different homes (foster homes) for two years until their house was rebuilt.

Through it all, Susanna was a great mom. She hated to be away from her children, and when they were all together in one house she made certain to spend one evening alone with each of them: Monday with Molly, Tuesday with Hetty, Wednesday with Nancy, Thursday with Jacky, Friday with Patty, Saturday with Charles. . . She educated them, taught them the Bible, kept the household running, and held Sunday prayer services in her house when her husband was away. Samuel felt it was wrong for a woman to lead services, but Susanna did it anyway.

You might think Susanna's strength and dedication as a good mother made her famous, but she is well known only because of her sons, John and Charles. The brothers are known for starting the Methodist Church. Charles also wrote the words to more than six thousand hymns.

In the worst of circumstances, Susanna trusted God and led her children to follow Jesus. She loved them and found time for each of them. She made her kids feel special. Do you know a mom like that?

. . . .

CHILDREN ARE A GIFT FROM THE LORD. THE CHILDREN BORN TO US ARE OUR SPECIAL REWARD.
PSALM 127:3

THE WIDOW OF ZAREPHATH
(1 KINGS 17:7–16)

Never-Ending Flour and Oil

The story of the widow of Zarephath found in the Old Testament happened during a famine—a time when food is hard to get. No rain had fallen for a long time, so all the crops dried up and died.

God said to His prophet Elijah, "Go to Zarephath. . .and live there. I have commanded a widow there to take care of you" (1 Kings 17:9 NCV).

When Elijah arrived there, he saw the widow gathering firewood. Elijah asked her for a cup of water. "Please bring me a piece of bread too," he said (1 Kings 17:11 NCV).

You might think it was a simple request, but the woman had only a handful of flour left in a jar and a little olive oil in a jug. She planned to use what she had to cook one last meal for herself and her son. When she told this to Elijah, he said not to worry.

He told her, "Go home and cook your food. . . . But first make a small loaf of bread from the flour you have, and bring it to me. . . . The LORD, the God of Israel, says, 'That jar of flour will never be empty, and the jug will always have oil in it, until the day the LORD sends rain to the land'" (1 Kings 17:13–14 NCV).

The widow of Zarephath went into her house and made a little loaf of bread for Elijah. She had plenty of flour and oil. The jar and jug kept filling up, and every day the woman, her son, and Elijah had enough to eat.

God always meets the needs of His people. When you read your Bible, you will discover His blessings from beginning to end. Don't worry—He will meet your needs too!

"I WILL ANSWER THEM BEFORE THEY EVEN CALL TO ME. WHILE THEY ARE
STILL TALKING ABOUT THEIR NEEDS, I WILL GO AHEAD AND ANSWER THEIR PRAYERS!"
ISAIAH 65:24 NLT

THE WIDOW WHO GAVE TWO MITES
(MARK 12:41–44; LUKE 21:1-4)

She Gave Everything

Are you saving your money for something you really want? Saving often means sacrificing—giving up other things. What if you had just enough saved up, and then God asked you to give it all to Him. Would you?

In Jesus' time, the Jewish temple had a special money box where people put their gifts to God. You might think of it like the offering plates passed in churches today.

Jesus sat in the temple watching people put money into the box. He saw rich people giving a lot. Although their gifts were generous, the rich had plenty left over. They gave to God only what they didn't need.

As Jesus sat there, He noticed a poor widow enter the temple. She pulled out two small coins and put them into the box. Back then those coins were called "mites." We can't know exactly what they were worth, but they were not worth much, especially when compared to what the rich people gave.

Jesus called His followers to come and sit with Him. He said, "I tell you the truth, this poor widow gave more than all those rich people. They gave only what they did not need. This woman is very poor, but she gave all she had to live on" (Luke 21:3–4 NCV).

No one but Jesus noticed the sacrifice this woman made. She gave God everything, all the money she had. Imagine what else she could have done with those two coins. Maybe they would have bought flour to make bread for a week. Was giving it all to God worth going hungry?

Jesus used this widow's story to teach His followers about true giving. She was willing to give everything to God.

Could you be that generous?

EACH MAN SHOULD GIVE AS HE HAS DECIDED IN HIS HEART. . . . GOD LOVES A MAN
WHO GIVES BECAUSE HE WANTS TO GIVE.
2 CORINTHIANS 9:7

Margaret Wilson
(1667–85)

Teen Martyr

Throughout history some Christians have given their lives to stay true to Jesus. The earliest were His disciples. They preached about Jesus and were put in prison and killed for encouraging others to believe. Many men and women have refused to deny Christ when others tried to force them to turn against their Savior. Those who choose to die instead of denying their faith are called "martyrs." Margaret Wilson was one of them.

She grew up a Presbyterian in Scotland during the 1600s, a time of much disagreement about who ruled the church. Citizens were expected to swear an oath that honored King James VII as the church's ruler. Refusing to take the oath meant death.

The Presbyterians wouldn't acknowledge the king as ruler of the church. Instead, they held secret meetings to practice their faith. If the Presbyterians were caught, the king's soldiers might kill them. As a teenager, Margaret attended these meetings with her younger siblings, Thomas and Agnes. None were willing to give in to the king's demands, so they worshipped in secret, sometimes hiding in the hills.

One day the king's soldiers captured Agnes and Margaret. Agnes was freed when her father paid for her release, but the soldiers kept Margaret in prison. When she continued to refuse to honor King James as head of the church, the soldiers drowned Margaret. But before she died, she prayed for the king's salvation, quoted the Bible, and sang hymns.

In the world today, many Christians are free to practice their faith and acknowledge Jesus as their Lord and Savior. But in many countries, Christians are still mistreated and even killed for their beliefs. It is important to remember them in our prayers and also to pray for everyone to accept Jesus so that someday they can live forever in heaven.

SO WHEN THE NAME OF JESUS IS SPOKEN, EVERYONE IN HEAVEN AND ON EARTH AND UNDER THE EARTH WILL BOW DOWN BEFORE HIM. AND EVERY TONGUE WILL SAY JESUS CHRIST IS LORD.
PHILIPPIANS 2:10–11

THE WOMAN AT THE WELL
(JOHN 4:4–15)

Living Water

On His way to Galilee, Jesus traveled through a mountainous region called Samaria. He arrived at a village named Sychar, which was built near a field. The women from Sychar went there to get water from a well.

Jesus felt tired from walking. He was thirsty when He noticed a woman at the well. "Would you give Me a drink of water?" Jesus asked.

She felt surprised when Jesus spoke to her. He obviously was a Jew. Jews didn't get along with people from Samaria. They avoided one another. So why was He speaking to her?

"Why are you, a Jewish man, asking me, a Samaritan woman, to give you a drink of water?" she asked.

Jesus had the perfect answer. "If you knew who I was, and if you understood how generous God is, then *you* would be asking *Me* for water."

The woman must have looked confused.

"I would give you fresh, living water," Jesus continued.

Living water! What was that?

"This well is very deep," said the woman. "And you don't even have a bucket to draw this. . .living water."

Then Jesus said something that must have confused her even more. "Everyone who drinks from this well will be thirsty again. But the living water I give will fill you up so you will never be thirsty—and it will give you forever life."

"Sir," the woman said, "then give me this water!"

"Living water" was Jesus' way of giving the woman a hint of what was to come. Later, after He died for our sins, anyone who trusted in Jesus would be filled with God's Spirit (Jesus compared it to "living water") and have the promise of never-ending life in heaven.

What about you? Would you like some living water?

"FOR GOD SO LOVED THE WORLD THAT HE GAVE HIS ONLY SON. WHOEVER PUTS HIS TRUST IN GOD'S SON WILL NOT BE LOST BUT WILL HAVE LIFE THAT LASTS FOREVER."
JOHN 3:16

THe WOMaN WHO ANOINTeD JeSUS' FeeT
(LUKe 7:36–50)

❧⁓⁓⁓❧

Forgiven!

Imagine going to a friend's house and being greeted with a foot washing! You are invited to sit. Your friend gets a basin of water, washes your feet, dries them, puts perfume on them, and then gives your feet a kiss! That seems crazy, doesn't it? But in Jesus' time, foot washing was a sign of hospitality. Think about it: People traveled mostly by walking. They wore sandals, and their feet got filthy and smelly. Washing someone's feet showed loving-kindness.

An important man invited Jesus to his house for dinner. A woman in the village knew that Jesus was there, so she arrived—likely uninvited. (The important man called her a sinner.) This woman loved Jesus, and when she saw Him, she cried. Her tears wet Jesus' feet, so she dried them with her long, beautiful hair. She brought with her a jar of her best perfume. She put it on Jesus' feet and then kissed them.

The man who invited Jesus to dinner felt disgusted. He thought if Jesus knew she was a sinner, He would have sent her away.

Jesus knew what the man thought. He knew what the woman was thinking too. She was Jesus' friend, and she felt in her heart that Jesus would die soon. That's why she cried and put special perfume on His feet.

"When I got here, you didn't wash My feet, put perfume on them, or kiss them," Jesus said to the man. "This woman loves Me, and her sins are forgiven."

Those at the dinner party wondered who gave Jesus authority to forgive a person's sins. They didn't know yet who Jesus was, and that soon He would be the only one with the God-given authority to forgive someone's sins.

Ask Jesus, and He will forgive your sins too.

• •

IF We TeLL HIM OUr SINS, He IS FaITHFUL aND We CaN DePeND ON HIM
TO FOrGIVe US OF OUr SINS. He WILL MaKe OUr LIVeS CLeaN FrOM aLL SIN.
1 JOHN 1:9

THE WOMAN WHO TOUCHED JESUS' COAT
(MATTHEW 9:20–22; MARK 5:25–34; LUKE 8:43–48)

"If Only I Can Touch Him"

Jesus did many miracles while He lived here on earth. Sick people heard Jesus had power to heal, so they came from all around to be cured. Wherever He went, crowds followed Jesus. Some people followed because they wanted a miracle. Others followed just to see what Jesus would do.

He was on His way to heal the sick daughter of a very important man. In the crowd that pressed around Jesus was a woman who had been sick for twelve years. She had bleeding somewhere in her body. This woman had tried everything to be healed. No doctor could help her, and she spent all her money on medical bills. Jesus was her final hope.

She believed she needed to touch Him to receive healing. The woman pushed her way through the crowd. She finally got close enough to touch His coat, and when she did she felt in her body that she was healed!

"Who touched Me?" Jesus asked. How did He know? Many had been pushing up against Him as they walked.

The woman felt afraid. Jesus and everyone following Him stopped. They all looked at her when she bowed down before Jesus and confessed, "It was me."

Jesus had pity on her. He spoke to her kindly, "Daughter, your faith has healed you. Go in peace and be free from your sickness" (Mark 5:34).

Did you notice that Jesus said, "Your faith has healed you"? Although the woman pushed her way through the crowd to physically touch Jesus, it wasn't the act of touching Him, but instead her faith in Him that brought healing.

If you need something from Jesus, you don't have to do anything special. Just have faith in Him. Ask, and then trust Him to provide whatever help you need.

KEEP A STRONG HOLD ON YOUR FAITH IN CHRIST.
1 TIMOTHY 1:19

courageous girls love god!

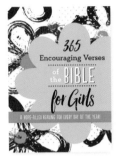

365 Encouraging Verses of the Bible for Girls

Every day for an entire year, girls will be encouraged, challenged, and inspired with great passages of scripture—addressing themes of God, Jesus, heaven, love, miracles, wisdom, and much, much more. Each devotional reading will meet girls ages 8 to 12 right where they are—offering words of comfort, peace, and hope for everyday life.

Paperback / 978-1-68322-348-1 / $7.99

How God Grows a Girl of Grace

Featuring 180 devotional readings complemented by easy-to-understand scripture selections and prayers, this delightful collection offers a powerful blend of inspiration, encouragement, and godly guidance for girls ages 8 to 12. Girls will be motivated to spend one-on-one time with God as they read about topics that are important to them.

Paperback / 978-1-68322-322-1 / $4.99